A Flame of
FIRE

A Flame of

A Story of My Own Identity and What It,
Means to Be a Minority in Iran

Khalil E. Nikkhessal

ARPress
ILLUMINATING IDEAS,
EMPOWERING VOICES

ARPress
45 Dan Road Suite 5
Canton MA 02021

| Hotline: | 1(888) 821-0229 |
| Fax: | 1(508) 545-7580 |

Ordering Information:

Quantity sales. Special discounts are available on quantity purchases by corporations, associations, and others. For details, contact the publisher at the address above.

Printed in the United States of America.

ISBN-13:	Softcover	979-8-89356-436-5
	eBook	979-8-89356-435-8
	Hardcover	979-8-89356-437-2

Library of Congress Control Number: 2024904011

To Farahnaz, the best faithful wife in the world, and my lovely children, Pedram, Pooneh, and Pegah.

In the world, there is only one virtue, that is knowledge and wisdom, and only a sin that is ignorance and nescience. (The great mystic Rumi)

Illustrations

Contents

Sixth Chapter

Preface

Humankind is made up of a series of memories both good and bad. It is made of joys and sorrows, successes and failures, and each memory is its own story. Although some memories are beautiful, they can be heart-wrenching as well. According to the observations, experiences, and things that happened the people who take advantage of any good opportunity and use it can be successful. However, if they do not take advantage of their opportunities, it will be a loss from which they can't regain. There are opportunities for everyone in their lifetimes, no matter how powerful or powerless they are. These opportunities will be dependent on their intelligence and understanding on social and political conditions and on geographic location. That means success is fifty-fifty, the first half is what we want, and the other half is how we use what we have. However, we should always take the lessons of our past, good or bad, into the future. We have to learn from the stones that are thrown, build firm steps for progress, aim to be successful, and try to stay on top. Success requires self-confidence, intelligence, and good circumstances. These things can be found in any situation if one is willing to work. There is no elevator to success, you have to go up the stairs. I remember a lot of emotional and physical trauma that, even today, I cannot describe. It has left me permanently fatigued and pain. These memories have paved the way for me.

This book is a collection of my stories and experiences. I always told myself that the hardships would pass, and I still say this even today. However, now I know that all the difficulties that have passed have been my life. The injuries are forever burned in my mind. Each of them is a fact of my life and defined my successes and failures, and these facts taught me how to trust others. I share my experiences with you now. Perhaps they can help you to discover the path to your own success. The first part is about early memories, education, and early work experiences. The second part describes the events of my life during the formative period of the Islamic Revolution of Iran. In the third part, I describe work-related issues, successes, and failures, as well as friendships, hatreds, and betrayals. As you will see, I draw no conclusions nor make any recommendations. These are merely my observations from the events of my life you may do with it as you would like. This is my story: *A Flame of Fire.*

Khalil E. Nikkhessal

Life is a series of memories, happiness, and hardship.
As we open our eyes, our life passes and ends.
We are all travelers and passersby.
Whatever has remained, just goodness!

A Flame of Fire

As we went up the stairs of the plane, I thought about what had happened. Why are we going to leave our native country forever? Many thoughts surrounded me, and I was confused. It was not our first trip that we took, but this trip had no return, and we were leaving our homeland forever. From a lifetime of worldly possessions, we were carrying only two suitcases each. We sat down, and the plane took off. I was still lost in thought when my wife told me that we had passed Iran's border. I felt as if I had been deported from my own country. My heart ached. I was depressed and sad and disappointed with much of life. We had to build a new life in a new country with a different culture and language. We were no longer young, and we did not have youth's ability for careless or even calculated risk. However, we also had no choice. If my brother had not helped us, we would never have been able to make the trip.

My wife and I had to stay in Vienna for a while. It took time for Austria to prepare a visa that would allow us to United States of America. I was severely fatigued from the stress of leaving Iran and it was a good opportunity to rest and relax. My brother and his wife had lived in Salzburg for a long time. They were waiting for us when we arrived at the airport in Vienna. I was very happy to see them. We all went to my brother's house in Salzburg.

Figure 1—My brother Djalil and I in Salzburg - Austria. (2011)

Salzburg is an old town with gorgeous green plains that are peppered with small lakes. It is the birthplace of Mozart. My brother's house sat atop a hill with a magnificent view of a green plain dotted with sycamore trees and a distant lake.

We stayed with my brother for about a week and then went on to Vienna where the U.S. embassy was located. We had to stay there while we waited for our visas. On June 2011, we boarded a plane headed for the United States.

Looking back, I realized at one point, something inside me changed at that moment. I had been betrayed and oppressed, but there was something new in my soul. A fire sparked within me; my determination built as we flew from Europe to the United States that no matter what I had suffered, I was going to live.

First Chapter

My Early Memories

Recalling the memories are often sad no matter good or bad. Even in my distant memories of childhood, because of my religion, I had always had a problem with fanatical Muslims. I was often teased and tormented by these zealots for my religion when I walked home from school. At that time we lived in Yazd, where the local Muslim community was largely illiterate, highly religious, and often superstitious in their interpretations of Islam. Even though I left Yazd after only fifth grade, my memory of it burns. I already knew something of the danger of religious zeal and religious-based malice from reading various books and listening to Bahá'í's history. In Yazd it was not unheard of for the Bahá'í to be tortured or killed. I can only say that ignorance and unwarranted prejudice is the only thing that makes a man worse than a wild animal.

People who can find love are able to help each other live in peace and freedom. People, who have twenty-five hundred years of culture, and also have known themselves to be part of the heritage of the Cyrus Charter of Human Rights.

I was an eleven-year-old kid when we moved to Shiraz. However, I had enough bad, sad, and traumatic experiences there to burn the Yazd community in my mind. My mother was sick with asthma. My father should go to an unknown city for many reasons such as his faith.

Figure 2—Upside: Uncle Dr. Kianoosh–grandfather–father Sitting: Mirza Waly Uncle Fethullah (insane)

My mother and I were lonely in this city full of wolfish people. I will never forget one scene in particular. Once, when I came back home from school, tired of the wicked children teasing me in the alley as I passed them, I saw my mother with a white handkerchief tied on her head and my older sister crying and holding a syringe. She was injecting my mother's upper arm. After a while, my mother's breathing became quiet, and the color of her face was white as snow. Then she went to sleep.

Our maternal uncle would take care of us, often coming to our house, but my elder brother worked for him. My brother had to wake up early each morning, wash the clothes, and dry them with a flat iron. It was a very hard work for a young sixteen-year-old schoolchild. After this work ended, he had to go to school. One day, my brother came home from school with a bruised face, wounded hands, and with a broken bike. On the way from school to home, several fanatic Muslim youths had beaten him and broken his bike.

My uncle (my father's brother) was living with us. He had been mentally disabled from a blow to the head as a child, and we took care of him. According to my father's tales, at the time of Qajar rule, the local mullah had encouraged some of the religious fanatics to kill my grandfather. When my infant uncle was breastfeeding from his mother, they raided my grandfather's home and hit him on his head hard enough to knock him comatose. The effect of this injury damaged his mental functions. My grandfather, in a feminine disguise, went underground to a neighbor's house through a stream channel and ran away. However, the locals looted all the belongings of his home.

My uncle liked my mother very much, and she was the only person he would obey. He rarely went alone out of the house because he would be teased so mercilessly that he would be upset for days. I remember one day he went out, dressed in women's clothing and makeup, and was teased and laughed at mercilessly. One of our neighbors saw him and brought him home. My mother was very upset, and cried for hours. Finally, when he was forty-three and we could no longer take care of him, he drowned in a creek in Yazd.

Figure 3—My Grandfather

My grandfather was a businessman who had a Clock shop in the Bazaar of Yazd. People called him Sir Sayed Mohammad Baqer, the watchmaker. He was the child of Aqa Sayed Zayn al-Abidine Behbahani, a famous cleric in Shiraz, who he was one of the appointed to the court of the Safavid dynasty and finally to Imam Hussein[1] and Fatemeh Sultan Kazerouni the granddaughter of Mohammad Taghi

---

1   Imam Hussain, a grandson of Prophet Muhammad and the third leader of the Shiite Muslim in the world.

Imam Quli Khan. He was the son-in-law of Shah Abbas Safavid and the governor of Fars.

As a teenager, he converted to the Bahá'í faith and moved to Yazd. His family was very close to the Afnans (the Afnan family was about Syed Ali Muhammad of Bab and they were very prominent and influential in Yazd and Shiraz). He married the daughter of the great trader of textile fabrics Meshkin Baf and had five sons and four daughters. He visited Bahá'u'lláh with a convoy on foot or by a horse in Acre. This was the only way to make the journey. The city of Acre was in what was then Palestine and was a big prison, which belonged to the Ottoman Empire (current Turkey). The holy family is imprisoned there. Today the city of Acre is in Israel. Hazrat Abdul Baha, the eldest son of Bahá'u'lláh, was connected with my grandfather, there are many tablets and letters that came from Acre. He was popular and respected as one of the people's favorite. The people liked him because he was very frank, honest, and has a friendly demeanor. He knew very interesting proverbs and jokes, and more importantly, he knew where he could use them. He knew when to talk about the new faith and ideas, and he had often done it. Because of this, most of the mullahs disagreed with him, and eventually even issued his death warrant.

Another uncle[2], my grandfather's first son was an intelligent man who was fascinated by the Arabic language and had beautiful handwriting (below). When he was a teenager, at the schoolhouse, his classmates badly wounded his neck with a knife. In those days, schools weren't like today's schools, but rather were held in private homes where students learned only religious education and Quran lessons and the teacher was a mullah. After three days of excruciating pain and profuse bleeding, he died at only sixteen years old. The night before his death he dreamed that he saw a holy man who lifted him from his bed and told him that he would be released, he told his dream to his father and died shortly after. Hazrat Abdul Baha sent in his honor a detailed tablet[3] referring to the dream. This tablet is too long and cannot bring it here, but the origin of it exist.

---

2   Figure 4 My uncle at fourteen years old. He was wearing the official clothing during the Qajar period in Iran.

3   This tablet is too long and cannot bring it here, but the origin of its exist.

Figure 4—My uncle Abdol Azim

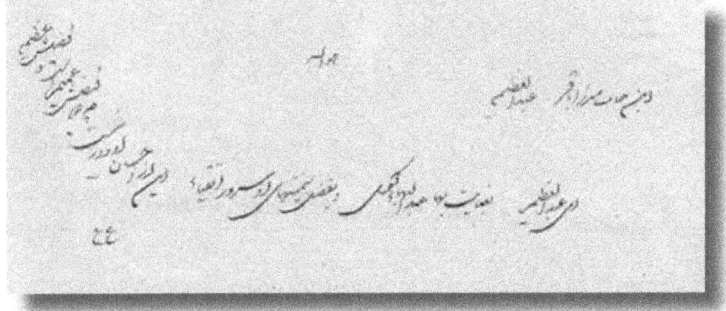

Figure 5—A small tablet which was sent from Abdul Baha before his death. (The original handwriting of Abdul Baha in Farsi)

O Abdul Azim, of Baha's kindness you will be AbdulBaha, and of his endless gracious to be chief of believers. It isn't far from his mercies, which is massive his bounty and has such a great grace.

Abdul Baha

Figure 6—English translation of the above tablet.

Before we moved to Shiraz and until fifth grade, I went to a Zoroastrian elementary school called Khosravi School, which was near our home. This school was run by a Zoroastrian Association and taught children who had different religions and upbringings more than just Islam. However, there were still a large number of Muslim children who were from intolerant families. Zoroastrian and Jewish children had their own religious studies, with their own religious texts, but

5

Bahá'ís and Muslims had to study Quran and Islamic religious classes together. Whenever I would read the Quran incorrectly, my teacher would smack me on the back of my neck and tell me I should eat hay (usually an animal food) and read the Quran more. He was not a fanatic like some of the other Muslims around me, but he said that I should have more respect for the Islamic teachings.

Each day when I walked to school, I would have to walk past a small market, which had some fruit grocery shops and a butcher shop. I remember running from the beginning of the market to the end past the shopkeepers who would tease me unrelentingly. I was always horrified of that market. By the time I was in Khosravi School, my brother had long since graduated and gone on to high school, Markar High School, which was also run by the Zoroastrian Association. However, the high school was much farther from our house, and my brother had to ride to school on a bike. On the way to and from, he was often intercepted by the fanatical Muslim youth and beaten up as well as having his bike broken or stolen. Sometimes he had to walk to school, and from time to time he even returned home barefoot.

Although I was born in the city of Yazd, I do not have any good memories of it. We did not have even a single day of comfort. Rather, our life was frequently one of anguish. I was there until the end of the fifth grade when after many years, my father was hired by a construction company as an accountant in the city of Shiraz, and he moved there to work. After a while, we also moved to Shiraz. We never went back to Yazd again.

Background

God has created humans as equal, but nobody said into what conditions each human is then placed. Humans have the influence of their surroundings and education on their thoughts, and each different background can lead to a different kind of personality. One is peaceful and merciful, another is cruel and torturous. One is a scientist who helps others, another becomes illiterate, superstitious, and destructive. Sometimes, these forces are so inexorable and powerful that they exert an irresistible force over people who live under them their whole lives. Cultures living for centuries under the pressure of superstitious thoughts are shaped by these forces and generations after generations treat their bigotry and superstitions as normal. How could anyone, in a few days or even a few years, hope to change

> There are people who live within cultures that for centuries have been accustomed to the religion and its right and lived with the name of God and my religion, the people who could not hear and learn anything else, above all, were kept illiterate with the new world is completely alien[4]. How can we tell them that there is another thought apart from what they think? They cannot understand you and hear your comments because contrary to what has been heard and acted, it is normal to react. They are superstitious and uneducated, therefore, they react to do every action, even murder. In particular, they have believed this concept and stressed that they should fight and kill the dissidents (means jihad). If they have been killed, they will enter the house of immortal and companioned with nymphs.

---

4   The people of Iran, before Reza Shah's time, had no birth certificate or identification card, and there were no schools and universities, only private Holy Quran classes.

Their minds or their mindset? It would take multiple generations beginning with re-educating the children to hope to undo these kinds of social forces. Let us think a little bit more about it, here I do not want to evaluate, research or study, which includes several books. Just to clarify your minds, why did the people behave in such a way? The history of Iran has been full of ups and downs, it may be like the history of every other country. Iran has been a special occasion5, it was always in different attacks and still is. The Aryans have a special property that is either black or white, gray are seeing less (moderate) when the Arabs occupied Iran. The people of Iran at that time were predominantly with the culture far richer than the Bedouin Arabs. They lived with their customs and urban life. Whether or not with the new religion (Islam), they brought it under pressure, I don't know. Arabs had forced the women to stay at home under strict rules of patriarchy. Arabs burned libraries and books. The book was only the divine book. Listening to music was banned, as well as having and playing musical instruments. Thus, the people experienced double life[6] and became accustomed to it. As a result, "lying" spread and this dichotomy will continue. Moreover, having one after another authoritarian regime with mullah's thinking and patriarchy and having a marjah (references emulation) or ayatollah (divine verses), a wise man who knows everything, and the other people do not know. He must decide for all the people and say what they should do or not do, and his followers should obey him. That was the biggest mental and thinking trauma on worn Iranian people's body, and unfortunately still is. People just listened to the words of the mullahs and ayatollahs, and their rules should be implemented[7]. Now, after a thousand and four hundred years having imitation thinking and being superstitious, once someone comes and tells them what you think is not right and the mimic is a superstition. Tell them, the equality of rights for men and women, universal peace, and religion should be based on reason and science, and you must put the guns down. Also, live with love and peace! You should be friendly

---

5   For more information refer to History of Iran After Islam by doctor Nasser Engheta.

6   Indicates the kind of behavior at home and outside the home is completely different.

7   For better understanding of the laws of the mullahs, refer to each of the books *Hallol Masa'il (Resolving the Problems)* written by any of the ayatollahs.

to everyone! Your life is for you with your decisions! Having a religious marjah is outdated. It is obvious, they would massacre the followers of these ideas and dissidents[8].

In Iran and Yazd where I was born, the people were superstitious, uneducated, and quite religious. Now, I don't know. It is normal that the people do not realize those thoughts at that time and doing unsavory actions. Particularly, mullah's influence and their opposition, for their interests were threatened. They had driven the people to revolt against dissidents because they were well able to take advantage of the illiterate and superstitious people. People, like mirror, reflected the image of mullahs in themselves, and really, they had no will of their own. In the name of God and religion "Jihad against infidels" and began to do all kinds of crime[9]. Here, I do not want to say something's good or bad about faith, creed, or ethnicity. I just wanted to give a background about the people who have no will to act and follow the instructions, those who do not think about anything except their personal interests.

It is the fire, which was kindled hundred plus years ago, from this idea has arisen, and the flame of this fire to the year 1979 Iran revolution has been stretched and is still ongoing. I am one of those flames who burned and grew up so I could fly in the skies and fade.

---

8   For more information refer to *History of Yazd Martyrs* written by Master haji Mal Amiri

9   For more information refer to "Nabil History" (Early history of Babis and Baha'is) written by Nabil Akbar.

Living in Shiraz

Shiraz totally changed our lives. Shiraz people were amenable, carefree, and happy-go-lucky, opposite of that was Yazd where people are hardworking and extremely religious. In Shiraz, we began a quiet life, we children all went to school because our parents cared about our education and said that we should all be higher educated in order to build a better future for ourselves. We had financial hardship therefore we moved into my aunt's house, and this was much more comfortable than in our own house in Yazd. We had a room in my aunt's house and shared the kitchen. My brother and I lived with my father in his workplace in a room. During the weekends we were with my mother and sisters. After a while, my father leased an apartment near his work and we all moved there. We had been very happy that we were all together. By the way, I have forgotten to mention that my eldest sister was married in Yazd and she lived with her husband in Tehran and at that time had one son. We had continued our life as normal in Shiraz, and our financial situation was getting better day by day. Many people trusted my father, and he continued his work as an accountant to solve their financial problems, and he was famous for providing good service.

I remember when we still lived at my aunt's home, somewhere, I saw a picture of a Venus statue, and I became familiar with the works of Michelangelo, the famous Italian painter and sculptor. I had read some books about him. I was very interested in making a statue of Venus. I decided I would try during the summer holidays, which would make it feasible. So at my aunt's house, in the backyard with bricks and stones together, I made a blank rectangle surface about one meter in height, and I filled it with gypsum slurry and left it for two or three days to dry out. After I picked up the bricks and stones, a square of plaster about 30 cm × 30 cm had formed over a meter

Figure 7—My Mother and Father

long. Then I started to lathe and trim it; I only had a knife and a brush as tools. Everyone laughed at me and did not believe I could do this job. Everyone was discouraging me except my brother who said if I would be able to complete the statue, then he would buy me a nice prize. During my three- month summer vacation with strange perseverance finally I made the statue, which was about my height. My family and friends were all very surprised that I did such a good job. My father used to always talk about it and praised my persistence. My high school period was a good time, in the summer holidays I worked, and I enjoyed it. There was a large and beautiful home in a very nice area of Shiraz whose owner was a Zoroastrian, when he is not in Iran, my father was responsible for it. The U.S. Army rented the house for officer's quarters. Because my father did not know any English, I did all the paperwork and was responsible for solving their problems and eventually I became friends with them and we had communicated with each other and sometimes I worked there as an interpreter.

My eldest brother, with his friend, went to Austria to continue his study. He was going to study medical science at the University of Innsbruck in Austria. After a while, my father bought a land in a good neighborhood in Shiraz, and little by little he built a house there. In the interim, my other sister got married when I was in my senior year of high school. She went to Tehran to live with her husband. After graduating from high school, I went to Tehran to participate in the nationwide university entrance exam for the Technical University of

Tehran. I always wanted to become an electrical engineer. Unfortunately, I was not   successful because the exam was very difficult and many young applicants who participated in the entrance exam did not pass the exam. The number of universities in Iran was limited at that time, and the number of students who wanted to go to the university was very large. Most of the students who passed the exam had taken it several times to succeed. Therefore, I had to wait a year and try another time.

Tehran is a big city with all its apparent beauty and it was attractive for an inexperienced young man like me. I stayed there on the pretext that I would find a better job. I could not find any good jobs because I did not have any experience and I did not want any ordinary jobs. I met with a friend who was working in an advertising company. I became interested in advertising and we established an advertising company together. It was my first mistake. My friend was a clever person and I was inexperienced. After a while, I had lost all my money and he owned all the company. I was very upset and suffered from the embarrassment of telling my father. My father came to Tehran and took me back to Shiraz. We decided in Shiraz that I travel to Germany to continue my studies, which was close to my brother. I prepared for my trip to Germany. I had heard many good things about Germany and I was very happy that I was going to a new country.

Start Gaining New Experiences

In Shiraz, I was ready for the trip to Germany and have done all the preparations necessary for the trip including purchasing a plane ticket. First, I had to travel to Tehran by bus and from there I could fly to Germany. When I was on the plane to Germany I had an interesting imagination. I looked out of the plane window. I saw a wonderful sunset view. On this amazing view, I saw an imaginary picture of my parents, they were saying goodbye to me. My father said to me, "My dear, you are going to another country with another culture. You have to be careful of yourself." Suddenly I became very sad. I was lonely and the sunset that I saw from the plane's window was so wonderful at this moment of my sadness. My loneliness and the beauty of the blood orange painted sunset, and the quiet sea underneath the plane, added to my gloom. It was so beautiful and exciting that I couldn't describe it. I was in those thoughts when I arrived at Munich Airport, and from there I took a taxi to the Munich Central Railway Station where I had to buy a ticket for the train to go to Manheim, where my brother was waiting for me.

The railway station was a very large place because most people in Europe travel by train more than by car. I saw many people who were in a rush. I was standing there with a lot of luggage. I neither knew the language nor someone who could help me. Inside the traveler sections at the train station, there were about twenty-eight train platforms and each platform had two tracks. On each track the trains moved and stopped about ten to twenty minutes. Finally, after searching with high stress, I bought the ticket, and I boarded on the train. I remember when I was on the train, I was so anxious and worried that all of my clothes had been soaked with sweat. Due to these difficulties, I became more responsible and independent to solve all of my problems alone for the first time. I was very happy for this success and independence.

When I was in Germany, the new problems and difficulties began. First, to learn the language, the second I had to gain admission to the University of Frankfurt, and the most difficult part was to stay there and continue my studies in German language and culture. However, I resolved most of my problems with patience and perseverance and spent hours and hours in consistent training. At first, I went to the Goethe Institute to learn the German language. Then I started to apply for different universities in Germany. I was admitted to Frankfurter Technical University on the condition that I pass the minimum six months experience in different sections as experiment student in a factory, and complete the two pre- semester (only for international students). I began to work at first in an electrical shop, I was installing electrical wiring in buildings until I found a place for training.

Prior to this, when I arrived in Germany, my brother found a room for me at his friend's home in a small town near Mannheim. He also found me a construction job. I had been working on this job for about a month. I remember perfectly well, the first day at work for me was extremely difficult. I stayed at the back of the moving belt which moved the bricks and stacks to the second floor of the automatic runway. It was a labor-intensive job and I had no time to rest. It was an easy job for other crew members but not for me. On the other hand, fifty pound-cement bags had to be loaded from the truck and I could not even move them. When I came home that day I was so exhausted that I stayed in bed for five days and I had to go to the doctor who prescribed me some pain medications. After five days, I went back to work again, and I started out with very simple tasks. I gradually became stronger in this job and at the end, I was able to lift a bag of cement, take it on my back, and carry it to the second floor. While working in construction, an interesting thing happened to me. Once a bee stung my hand and my hand became swollen, it looked too large and unusual. That day I was very angry, and I thought that everyone looked and laughed at me, while nobody was really paying any attention to me.

My brother was proud of my tolerance during this period because he was my sponsor and adviser. I had passed his tests, I was glad that I accepted the construction job and did it well. "No pain, No gain." There were no parents around, and I had to do and handle everything by myself.

University on the condition that I pass the minimum six months experience in different sections as experiment student in a factory, and complete the two pre- semester (only for international students). I began to work at first in an electrical shop, I was installing electrical wiring in buildings until I found a place for training.

I found a training place in the Brown Boveri & Cie (BBC) factory in Manheim, and I was working there as a trainee for six months and learned a lot. The BBC was a huge factory, they were building all sorts of things, from household appliances to power plants. I was working in different parts of the factory every two weeks. The first three weeks I worked in the section of trainings, lathing, and filing. Then I began working in the transformer division where they built large transformers for power plants. There was an old man, whom I worked with, and I learned a lot from him. I remember a day he gave me a crooked pipe that I had to paint. When I painted it, he looked at me and said, "My son, you should learn to do it right, it doesn't matter what it is. The inside of the pipe is not painted, here in Deutschland things needs to be perfect." I visited many parts of the factory. I learned how they carefully polished huge steam turbine engine blades. Finally, I worked in the electronics design division and electronic parts. I learned how to work electronic parts when they were working together in a planning process. I think I learned in the short term more than all the things that have learned in my life so far. That was an amazing and exciting period of my life.

My pre-semester classes were held in Giessen. Giessen was a university town where there were many students who came from all over the world to study in colleges, institutes, and universities. In Giessen, nothing important happened. In the two pre-semester we studied German language, mathematics, and a short term of chemistry and social rules in Germany. In Giessen, I found many friends and some of them are still in touch. I had a good time there, and I was very happy. Sometimes, I worked in a spaghetti factory to improve my financial situation. I lived there for one year and this period was one of the best moments and unforgettable times of my life. I went to Frankfurt to register at the Technical University, and I did what they required for admittance to the university.

My first day in the university was the most important and unforgettable day in my life. I will never forget that. The story began when I went into the classroom on the first day. I saw a very big place with more than hundred students in different year levels. Two teachers were standing in front of the hall with a microphone in hand and spoke. The other students had understood it, and they wrote it quickly, but I did not understand a single word, how could I write like them. I had become extremely depressed because I had learned the German language and I had finished two special pre-semester before I came here yet I did not understand any words, why? When I came back home tired and sad, I told my brother that I could never succeed in this class, and I could never understand and write quickly like the other students. My brother spoke to me about his difficulties and how he was able to solve his problems. First, he bought a small tape recorder to record the lessons. The next good advice, I should select the courses that does not require a lot of usage of languages, such as mathematics, physics, and other sciences.

The first and second semester were quite overwhelming. I had to spend hours and hours listening to the audio recording and I wrote about what I had understood.

Finally, in the third and fourth semester, I started to understand along with other students in the class. After six years of hard work in the university and two years before that in Giessen and Manheim, I finally graduated with a Master of Science degree (MS) in Electronics Engineering. While I was writing my engineering dissertation, I went to Iran and got married with my wife Farahnaz in the summer holiday of 1970.

Figure 8—Our Wedding

During my studies, I always had worked mostly in (Allgemeine Elektricitäts Gesellschaft) AEG- Telefunken in Frankfurt. Earlier during the holidays, I worked as an urban train ticket seller. Then I found a job as an electrical map drawer in the division of research and development of power plants in AEG- Telefunken Frankfurt. I worked there during all my university holidays and from two to six p.m. every day after my classes except Saturdays and Sundays. After my graduation, I worked as an electrical engineer in Frankfurt Airport. It was a very good job but I lost it because of a Palestinian terrorist action that happened in Munich Airport. Most of the foreign employees, especially from the Middle East, were laid off. Then I worked for Tracor Inc. as a service engineer, and finally, I found a job as a design engineer in T&N a related company to AEG and I worked there for two years.

AEG Company at that time won a bid for all electrical work in Kish Island in Iran. I was among those who went to Iran to perform electrical work in several large buildings and make a power plant in that region. I was there for a year, I worked in power plant design. When I returned to Germany, they offered me a job in AEG-Iran and I accepted and went to Iran to stay and work permanently in Iran. This was my biggest mistake.

A German proverb says, "Not every day is Sunday." That year was so good to me. First, I was a visitor and my family often invited me to parties. Second, as a designer and consultant, I was constantly traveling from Frankfurt to Tehran and Kish. Since I lived and worked permanently in Iran, those family interactions became less and less, and this case would not be identified in a temporary life and job. That was my second mistake. Maybe not, I do not know.

After living in Tehran for some time, I changed my job and I went to Shiraz to work in Iran Electronics Industries as a design engineer in research and development division. Iran Electronics Industries was dependent on the defense industry of the Iranian Army. The Division of Research and Development was formed from many sections and I was working in the section of designing the Digital Private Automatic Branch Exchange (PABX). In the room where I was working there were twelve Iranian designers and five Americans, other than those who were in the lab and the printed circuit design. I worked there for about a year and a half and completed the project of PABX design when the revolution happened in 1979.

Second Chapter

Formation of the Islamic Revolution in Iran

When the revolution was taking shape, it refreshed my Yazd memories. In September 1979, we went on vacation to the Caspian Sea in the north of Iran, we had no news of the revolution and we knew neither Khomeini nor the other mullahs. On the way back from vacation, we saw some protests in some cities. There were protests also in Shiraz. The riots at Jaleh Square, shooting in Tehran, and the killing of innocent people was very sad, and the people had been leading to protests against the regime.

In summer of 1953, Prime Minister Dr. Mohammad Mossadegh rebelled against the Shah and he held protests in the streets and the people destroyed the statue of the Shah and everywhere there was the talk of the Shah fleeing the country. At that time, I was in fourth grade in Yazd. I remember well when I went to school in the mornings, there was a man who was moving against my direction and went to his work and in the afternoons when I came home from school, he was going home. One morning, I saw him shouting with a slogan "I wrote with my blood, either death or Mossadegh!" Another afternoon, I saw him on the street again, he was saying, "Long live the Shah, long live the Shah!"

I was a little boy and I did not know much about politics, I didn't understand and could not say which slogan was correct. However, I understood that something important had happened and changed people and their minds. They soon changed their opinion and that is just due to illiteracy and culture, they were fair-weather friends. I hope and wish that one day, we, Iranians, will think and gather more information before we make any movement or we accept or reject something. I do not have anything good or bad to say about the political movement, I was totally shocked to see the behavior of people. As a young kid I just needed to know how to act in this situation. Perhaps, one of the reasons for such thinking or behavior was a source of emulation (mullahs) and people were accustomed to letting the religious figures decide for them and if they were wrong, they would accuse the enemies. It is very dangerous and I didn't know why did the Iranian Revolution happened, and why the people set their country on fire without thinking about themselves and their family.

The BBC radio was always broadcasting the protests and gave them the necessary coverage. I first heard the name and voice of Khomeini from the BBC radio. Another tragic incident was the fire at Cinema Rex in Abadan, where one of the largest oil refinery in the world was located. Cinema Rex in Abadan was a beautiful place and at the time of the fire was filled with women, men, and children who were burned alive in the fire. Investigators of this horrific incident reported that all the doors had been locked, and the fire started in different places within the cinema on purpose. No one survived. They had burned all together, and from the cinema with all its audience only a hill of ashes had remained. This was a serious crime against humanity. For this horribly sad incident, the government declared a week of mourning.

Revolutionary propaganda devices and foreign radios announced that the regime had done this tragic event intentionally. The fact is that the regime did not benefit from it. This terrible incident angered the fanatic people and people began to set fire on government offices, banks, and some modern theaters (without spectators) in some cities. This incident led to strikes and protests by workers of Abadan Oil Company and in all the cities of Iran. Disruptions were almost in every city of Iran, and they all had listened to the BBC radio. Iranian National Radio and TV of Iran employees were on strike, and the military ran them. Curfew had been imposed in most major cities in Iran. National Iranian Oil Company employees were on strike. I could say, almost all major companies and factories were being shut down, but the food was abundant everywhere. Moreover, the protests were so easily and happily without the resonance and no shortage. I remember during the height of the formation of the Islamic revolution that there were protests in all the streets. Creating large categories and groups and slogans such as "Down with Shah" or other things and regularly moved forward. The employees of state organizations, factories, all companies, airlines and even the radio and television were on strike except grocery stores. My wife and my little son were in her parents' house in Tehran, I wanted to bring them to Shiraz but because Iran Air was on strike, I had to travel by bus at night. The next day I was in Tehran. In one of the major streets in Tehran, I do not remember which one, there were huge protests in motion and I had to wait for hours until we could continue our way. There were slogans and protests through loudspeaker and the demonstrators were repeating them.

All of a sudden the distance between protesters increased. The loudspeakers invited them to join and reunite again, people repeated the same sentence instead of doing what they were supposed to do. This showed that they're not using their brain, and they were just imitating without understanding.

People with cultural poverty are like a mirror that reflects only its target audience. It says a teacher went to a village to give the people an opportunity to learn literacy. The local mullah worried if the people become literate, they do not want more listen to him, and his business will be ruined. He was thinking of a remedy, and he started to spread words that the teacher is a liar, and he would take you away from religion and faith. So he should tell the truth, and he should take a literacy contest with me.

One day the mullah invited the teacher and the people to the local mosque, everyone gathered in the mosque. The mullah ask the teacher to write the word snake on the blackboard, and the teacher wrote the word snake. When it was the mullah's turn, he drew the shape of the snake on the board. Then the mullah looked at the people and said, "I want you people who live in this town to tell me which one of these shapes means snake." They all pointed to the drawing of the snake on the board and said that the mullah wrote it correctly. The actual teacher was considered a liar, was beaten up and driven out of town.

The moral of the story is that friendship with someone who is ignorant and illiterate is just uncomfortable and stressful. People, especially at that time, were mostly superstitious and uneducated. Unfortunately, we always blame others for what we have done. For example, say that foreigners have led the revolution in Iran. Why don't the foreigners in Switzerland or Sweden make revolution in those countries? The reason is that the people in those countries think before taking any actions. Unfortunately, we know ourselves as the best one, and never assess the consequences.

Another horrible incident happened in Shiraz, this regrettable event was at the Saadi neighborhood in Shiraz. It is an ancient village on the outskirts of Shiraz, it was called Saadi because one of Persia's famous poets Saadi's tomb is located there. Prior to this event, some Bahá'í families lived in Saadi village in peace with other religions. It began when a strong Bahá'í man who was working in the army lived there. He was very popular and had a lovely family and two beautiful young daughters. One night, at a mosque during Muharram, the mullahs provoked the people by saying that Bahá'ís are the enemies of the Islamic religion, and their blood is solvent, and if you kill them in this holy month, you will go to heaven. Muharram is an Arabic lunar month. This month the Islamic prophet's grandson, Imam Hussain, the third leader of Shiites, with seventy- two of his followers in Saudi Arabia became martyrs in the desert of Karbala. This month is sacred for Shiite Muslims, and they mourn for forty days. In this month, there is always the problem of religious minorities particularly the Bahá'ís were manifold because people were more sensitive and the mullahs could play with their emotions. During one of the mourning nights, the people were irritated, they went to the military man's home, began to insult him, his beliefs, and invaded his house, and they said, "Tonight your daughters are legit to us." He was frightened and defended his family, he tried to make people disperse and started to shoot with a hunting rifle, as a result, a few people were wounded. During this opportunity, his family could escape with sleepwear and with bare feet walked toward the mountain to the other Bahá'í house. However, angry fanatics and fools who wanted to go to heaven killed the military man atrociously, looted and burned his house.

The incident was a pretext to start a larger event. The next day, they began to regularly destroy and burned the homes of Bahá'ís. They started rumors everywhere that Muslims were killed by the Bahá'ís. In all the streets, the drivers were honking their horns that Ashura10 is repeating and Muslims have been massacred. Everywhere was filled with an atmosphere of fear and terror. They started to despoil and to burn the homes of Bahá'ís in Saadi and other places.

Then they began from the southern city of Shiraz; they had all information to the identification of the Bahá'í homes. Most of the Bahá'ís had left their homes and moved to another city or in the homes of neighbors. It was quite a frightening atmosphere, I constantly received a lot of news that they would have reached the home of this and that Bahá'í. I did not go to work and I did not know what to do. I and my wife and my little boy lived with my parents. My mother was sick but fortunately we lived in the north side of Shiraz which was quite.

All these events took place during the military rule in front of the soldiers. The government was silent and showed no reaction. I was extremely upset and drove on the streets to have more information about the situation and I told my wife that my mother and the others had to go my friend's home who lived nearby if necessary. It lasted three days and almost thirty percent of the Bahá'ís' homes had been robbed and burned. Then one of the most famous and influential clerics issued a statement saying that God does not forgive those who burn houses. Moreover, other people should be quiet, and they should not do anything more. The radio and local television broadcasted this message several times. After that, the city of Shiraz became quiet, but those memories will never be forgotten.

At that time I understood when people are ignorant how easily they can be influenced. Now I understand why the Shah could not fail to run the gates of civilization. The most important factor in the growth of a community is a society's culture. The public must be educated and

---

10   Ashura—a day of mourning by Shi'a Muslims for the martyrdom of Imam Hussain, the grandson of prophet Muhammad with a small group of his companions and family members at the Battle of Karbala on 10 Muharram in the year 61 AH (680 CE).

they are the ones making culture of the public, and it takes a lot of time. For example, several hundred years lasted to establish a secular culture in Europe. We are a nation that has lost its identity. I do not understand it—how we can give our children, the lovely Iranian kids, the name of one of the greatest enemies of Iran such as Genghis, Timor, and Alexander, or any Arabic names.

I remember in high schools they do not emphasize on history or literature. However, they were hard up in the religious studies or the holy book. It would help all the students become aware of their country's history. Also, the religion is a personal obligation and choice. If anyone would like to learn it, they can learn, but it should not be an important subject in high school. I think from the second or third grade in primary school we had to learn the Quran. It is funny that we learn and read like a parrot until the last year of high school, it means we read only the Quran and we never understood it, and no one translated it for us. Whose idea was it that students should not read history books but they must read religion and Arabian books? I do not know.

I think that Iran's Islamic Revolution in 1979 derived from this issue—Pahlavi's two most sworn enemies had been collated together. On one side was Dr. Mosaddegh's followers that were labeled nationalistic and intellectual and the other side were with the most religious fanatic and backward and cortical mullahs who were working with communists together to destroy Iran again. We saw how the clergy destroyed their comrades after the victory, one after another. According to a story, there were three people—one Mullah, a Syed[11], and an ordinary man went to a garden, and picked the fruits of the garden. The garden's owner saw them stealing and realized that he alone could not defeat the three men. He thought and came closer, and said to the ordinary man, "He is a mullah and we must respect him, and this person is Syed and a descendant of the Prophet, who are you?" He beat him and tied his hands and feet. Then he went toward Syed and said, "Here is our mullah and we should respect him. You had no right to pick my fruits without my permission," and he beat him too and tied up his hands and legs together. After that he came to the mullah and said, "You are a

---

11   The people who were born from the Prophet Mohammed generations.

mullah and should encourage others to do well, why do you come here to steal?" And he also beat the mullah, closes his legs and hands. The clergy used the same politics, with the help of these groups. They first used them to win and then destroyed them one by one.

In early 1970, with increased reliance on oil revenues, Mohammad Reza Shah created a series of programs to improve the country. In March, the plan White Revolution took place. This included land reform, an extension of voting rights to women, and the elimination of illiteracy, in addition to the major projects for the underlying structure of Iran. However, this social and economic development was caused increasingly by stimulation of the clergies. But more importantly, in 1971, Shah held the celebration of 2,500 years of the Persian monarchy. In 1976, he replaced the Arabian land reform, an extension of voting rights to women, and the elimination of illiteracy, in addition to the major projects for the underlying structure of Iran. However, this social and economic development was caused increasingly by stimulation of the clergies. But more importantly, in 1971, Shah held the celebration of 2,500 years of the Persian monarchy. In 1976, he replaced the Arabian calendar year 1355 with an "imperial" Iranian calendar year 2535, which began with the foundation of the Persian Empire over twenty-five centuries earlier. All of these amendments were too much for a nation that has been illiterate, superstitious, and lacked understanding. These actions have been viewed as un-Islamic and as a result formed an opposition that was ruled by the more religious clergy. The people who were illiterate were exploited by the clergymen and used them against the opposition.

The people of Iran before Pahlavi were in a leadership of the oppressive and tyrannical puppet governments, and extremism clergymen religious for a long time. All the people were accustomed to living in fear, a state of apathy and ambivalence in behavior, and had a habit of lying and superstition, and above all, they were illiterate. A new high culture and civilization require a breakdown and revolution. Mankind does not start with a loose culture, superstition, and illiteracy, and cannot build a civilized and cultured society with exalted thoughtful people. All these issues must first be erased from the minds of the people, and then with patience and passion, they should begin to build new cultural institutions. This requires several revolutions. Like other revolutions that took place in Europe. The thesis is a simple one. A modern tower building must have had a good and strong foundation, and you cannot build it upon an old and frail foundation.

Therefore, we conclude, this religious revolution for Iranian people was necessary to build a modern Iran, away from superstition. How long will it take? It depends on people's willingness to understand what is best for them. This revolution must happen. In some countries people understood it sooner and they found a solution to escape from it. Certainly the other revolutions are in the way, given that in this religious revolution happened a lot of transformations. European revolutions, it has taken from renaissance time to almost end of the nineteenth somewhat the twentieth century over five hundred years.

Currently, due to the Internet and world communication, history moves much faster. People are aware of other people in the world immediately, and they will be influenced by each other. Fortunately, at present in Iran, many people, especially the young people, are familiar with this phenomenon, and they have already used it. Currently, Iranian women, who constitute half the population, are more educated and there are more girls than boys in Iranian universities.

They work outside the home and have the right to vote. Although these incidents don't like the religious rule in Iran, the situation they are in forced them to silence and advance other issues, example Islamic veil and so.

Before the revolution happened, when we were still working, one day a young engineer—who was not a fanatic, was a friend, and was working in another part of the electronics industry—came to our workplace and told us, "The Bahá'ís say that your leader has declared that the Shiite clergy is a disgust and the people will hate them. Now, what do you say? You can see that every day the clergy are dearer and the people more respectful to them. Therefore, this is also another lie. My Bahá'í friend told him, "Wait! Why do you jump to conclusion unless you have not heard, that the slang said, a person who is very sick and he is going to die all of a sudden, he feels relief and better.

That is called "He brought the light to home[12] which means he will die soon." However, suddenly the motion stops and dies. Now the clergies brought the light to the home and continued to say, finally, the people should understand what creatures they are then the young man screamed and dashed out of the room with rage.

---

12   It is a term that is common among the people.

Third Chapter

Beginning a New Life in the Islamic Republic of Iran

Very soon after the revolution, as previously explained, they fired me because I had a different opinion. They thought that they would clear the area of astray people. It was not just I who lost the job, but they fired all the Bahá'ís of Iran. University professors, teachers, and hospital nurses, in short all Bahá'ís in all the places where they worked were fired. Not only had the people lost their jobs but also university students were expelled. It was a disaster for Iran's Bahá'í community. Therefore, everyone was trying to help others to the best of their abilities. It was a very hard decision when they did not have their own business, nor could they be employed in any place, and they did not have any hope for a better future.

The revolution changed all that. As I said, in our department there were twelve Iranians, five American designers, and only two Iranian Muslims. The rest were four Bahá'ís, three Jewish, two Zoroastrian, and one Christian. I was in charge of the design department. Before the revolution, the Americans left Iran. Then after the revolution, the Bahá'ís were fired from their jobs because of their religion. I and one of my Bahá'í friends stayed there because we were essential employees to the PABX design. A letter came from the Department of Defense that we had to continue our work, and we worked there until we completed the design. We had completed the design and I invited some university professors and prominent individuals in government in Tehran and Shiraz to a two-day seminar. During this seminar, we had shown the feasibility demonstration and how and what we had designed. Also, how the microprocessors could be used in the industry with programs that can be controlled and use the electronic memory in the circuit which can be executed by several instructions automatically (the Intel 8080A microprocessor was a recent phenomenon that we had used in our design). This seminar was highly regarded and was quite a successful seminar. The handout book of this seminar is available in the Iran Electronic Industry Library.

Later, I heard from a friend that if we did not resign, the fanatics of the regime would sabotage the company and show that we were the culprit. Immediately, I resigned and sent the letter of my resignation to the personnel department. In that letter, I said that I have completed my project and I cannot do more work there. I enclosed my identity card and I did not go back there again. I heard later that they were unable to continue the project. Given that I did all the design and also showed them the way to build it, I sent all of my design work to the manufacturing department and they still had them in the archive but they were not successful to build it.

A friend has told me that he had visited a factory in Poland. At that time, Poland was still a communist country. He asked his guide person, "I think this is an old factory, and it was built before the communist's time. What did you do with the owner or the person who made this factory?" The guide surprisingly said, "What should we have done with this fellow activist and entrepreneur person? Nothing! He still works in his former office, before he worked for himself and now for the nation."

However, in Iran the factory owners were executed or they fled abroad and they were called bloodthirsty and arrogant. Their factories and companies were seized, the lives of the owners were destroyed and their families were defamed.

There are many disputes here and it must be said that ignorance and superstitions are a very devastating disease.

Who did the revolution, the so-called educated people and their followers? For example, Reza Shah had sent Mr. Bazargan to France to be an engineer when he returned home to build his country. He came back, but he wrote a book about the water. The water is the amount of water in a pool with dimensions equal to about one meter (one cubic meter of water). Muslims believe that the water is always clean. He wrote in his book that if a dog drinks from our water the water will be unclean, but if a dog urinates in our water, the water is still clean, and we could get ablutions with it. Later, this kind of elite and intellectuals had led the revolution in Iran. They gave the country as a gift to the mullahs who were fanatics, bloody, and malicious like Khomeini. The people who had seen the picture of Khomeini on the moon, can you imagine it? It seems that those people were deprived of having a brain in their heads. This is a fact, and I was a witness in this matter. Our neighbor who was educated and a state employee came to our home at night in Shiraz and said, "I know you have a good remote camera, please lend it to me so I can better see my Sir Khomeini on the moon."

Establishing a Maintenance Company

I began as a self-employed repairman for electronic equipment. According to my past records and experiences, it was a good start for me, and I was able to hire some unemployed Bahá'ís. I opened my workshop at one of the rooms in my father's house for repairing the electronics equipment. I started by repairing electronic equipment for hospitals in Shiraz. Subsequently, the factories were also referred to us for repairing their machinery. During the revolution, the specialists in most of the factories were either fired and had left the country. It was a good opportunity to give service to them.

I remember a factory which was previously owned and run by the Japanese, during the revolution the revolutionaries had seized it. Since Japanese experts left Iran, the factory was shut down and the workers were laid off. This led them to ask me to set up the factory again. My technical colleagues including a Christian and a Jewish engineers and the others were all Bahá'ís at that time. We went there and worked hard and continuously. Finally, we were able to set up the factory again in three weeks. Therefore, all the laborers were able to work there again. On the reopening day of the factory, it was announced in the news on TV at night. "The factory (X) did not produce at all when the foreign experts left the country. Three engineers who are committed Muslims and experts began working again. Therefore, we handled our industry by our experts, and we did not need foreign experts."

For this reason, I was able to register my company in my own name. I started a successful business and I could employ a large number of Bahá'ís who were fired from their jobs. Shortly after, two of my fellow engineers moved from Iran, one to America and the other to Germany. They told me that Iran is not our place to live and they so insisted that I go with them, too, but I refused. I told them that my mom is sick and my company has been successful, and I have some employees who all have a family. If I leave the country, what will they do? Later I heard that they were very successful in their work and both were working in research centers. I was surprised at how the experts were fired in Iran and rehired immediately in foreign countries. In Iran Electronics Industries in Shiraz those experts who had several patents were fired too. My friend who was working on a laser project in Iran and was terminated but got involved in the same project in England, received an award from the Queen of England. Therefore, we were appreciative of our specialists.

I continued my work at home with electronics repair for hospitals and factories in Shiraz. I lived in my parent's house, which was on the ground floor, my family and I lived on the first floor. It was a big house. I had used one office and two large rooms on the ground floor as a workshop. I slowly became well known and various factories that had problems came to see me. I made two expert groups—one group, which I led, for hospitals to repair industrial machines. For Belfer Stone Cutting Factory we designed and made a numerical control device that could cut stones at length, width, and thickness to be determined automatically by the operator and for Hafiz Ceramic Tile Factory. Another machine for automatic packaging, for example, twelve tiles were removed and packed, and these twelve packets were put in a cardboard box and at the end of the day the number of tiles would be recorded. The number of tiles and number of the boxes could be determined beforehand too. Maybe you think it is easy, for now with programmable microcontroller, yes, but in Iran in the 1980s, it was something very special and difficult.

Another interesting event occurred early in the revolution when I had registered my company. A few days after our Bahá'í neighbor's son was arrested for no reason. Later he was martyred.

One day, two revolutionary guards armed with guns came to my workplace and said, "Which one of you is Khalil Nikkhesal?"

I said in surprise, "I am."

And they told me, "We must immediately go to Adel Abad prison together."

I was very scared because many people had been arrested and taken to jail. I said, "Can I tell my family?"

They said, "No."

I just told my colleagues, "Please tell my family and bring my son home from his elementary school."

Then I went with them to prison. When we arrived we went to the jail warden. He told me with respect, "Thank you for coming here so soon, part of our power generator does not work, and we want you to repair it. And we will pay whatever it costs."

I felt at ease and said, "Why did you bring me here with arms and now I am not ready because my family is worried about me." At the moment, I was not in a good mental condition. "I will come by tomorrow and I will repair the generator."

Then the jail warden told the revolutionary guards, "Why did you have this kind of behavior?"

They said, "You told us that we should bring him in here, and we brought him."

I immediately went home and the rest of that day I could not do anything. The next day I went to the prison, and I repaired the generators in which the electronic control was damaged. This was the same prison where my father and many of Shiraz Baháís were detained and still are. Some of them had been executed for the crime of being a Bahá'í.

There is a saying "the apple fell from the tree and the world became aware of the law of gravity." However, thousands of corpses fell yet no one understood the meaning of humanity. A very tragic and painful event happened in Shiraz. Ten young Bahá'í girls aged seventeen to twenty-three were executed on June 1983. They were in charge of being an ethics classroom teacher for Bahá'í children. This class was formed for the Bahá'í children only two hours in their homes on Friday morning, where the children were to learn Bahá'í ethics and virtues. They studied how to love others. The people love them, they learned to be honest and do the right thing and peace is sighted. Among them was a seventeen- year-old girl named Mona. The Islamic Revolution Court executed her due to her membership in the Bahá'í administration and Israeli spies. She was sentenced to death. Of course, since the 1979 Islamic Revolution, these Bahá'í martyrs were not the first and not the last. A lot of women and men who had the same charges were executed, like Mona's father and many others.

The court authorities did not release the trial decision to the accused families. However, the Shiraz Islamic Revolution trial judge, during an interview with Khabar Newspaper (official gazette in Shiraz), justified the executions. It was obvious that in the Islamic Republic of Iran there was no small place for Bahá'ís. He spoke of the people who had been sentenced to death as "Jihad ba Kuffar"[13] (fighting with the infidels) and added, "These people were sentenced to death, have been active members of the Bahá'í faith and the simple- minded people were not safe from the evil of them. Establish their dependence on the inside and outside demons and hostility toward Islam and Muslims."

The next day of testimony of the Bahá'í girls, the emotions in the city of Shiraz was different, in the eyes of all Bahá'ís in Shiraz were seen the tears and immense grief. I really cannot express the feeling and sadness of that day because the pen is incapable of understanding those feelings. In the survivors' homes was the rite of prayer and litany, and many people were commuting. Everywhere was a bowl full of Noggles[14], and other sweets were served to visitors. It seems and was believed, at that day, the city of Shiraz was full of ambiguity and sorrow. It was surely a tragic day. I remember in one of the martyr girls' homes, whom we had gone to commiserate, out of the entire family only a young girl had survived, she had lost her sister, mother, and father. Her sister was among the ten girls, and her parents were executed a

---

13   The mention of the atheists that live outside of the Islamic state and have no rights, even the right to live.

14   Noggle is a kind of deliciously fragrant white candy made of almonds or pistachios and usually served at the wedding ceremony, they shed this over the head of the bride and groom.

day before were. Before I came to America, I still had the sweets that I collected at that day.

Now, the cemetery where they were buried has been destroyed by the revolutionary guards and they built an Islamic Culture House on top of their bones. However, this location was a Bahá'í cemetery and is called Golestan Javid (Eternal Rose Garden), my mother was also buried there.

When a person thinks about the kind of adventures his life has had and what might be happening in the future, it seems to be difficult to believe all. However, it is our life. Whether we are interested in or we would like to live again. I could never imagine it, that I will start this from the beginning again. I am glad that the life has an ending.

I don't remember how long it was after the revolution. The Islamic committee15 detained my father on a trumped-up charge that my father sent money to Israel. I was in my father's court and the judge who was a bearded young man and could not sit on the chair well (he was sitting cross-legged on a chair) was judging death or freedom of people like my father. He was saying, "How could you be trusted by the twenty-six people who are different in faith and personality. Tell me, how much money have you sent to Occupied Palestine16?" When he saw and realized who I am, he yelled sharply and said, "Go out! Your breathing will pollute the air!" The sentence he had issued for my father was imprisonment and he sent an eighty-one- year old and a good man to Adel Abad Prison in Shiraz. After that, when I got home and opened the front door, I felt the side of my right eye was hot. Later, an eye doctor specializing in Tehran said that the tiny blood vessels in my right eye was under too much pressure and the nerves ruptured, they should be mended with a laser beam. He said, "This disease was previously mentioned in the medical books, but now it is very high and common." I had done everything that I could and had talked to all the people who I thought might have been useful to help for my father's release. One day, I went to see one of the most influential merchants in Shiraz market. After making an appointment and getting

15   Islamic Revolutionary Police.
16   The Islamic revolutionaries say to Israel "occupied Palestine." They believe that Jews have occupied the Palestinian lands.

the permission, I entered into his office. It was a large room with many people who were sitting on chairs around the room. I also saw a man with a white beard and a smiley face with the influential eyes who was sitting behind the table in the corner of this room. When I introduced myself, he stood up, and the others followed him. I was upset at his behavior because I was a young person, and he was an older gentleman. I said, "Please don't embarrass me further."

He told me, "I stand up for your father because he is a very honorable person."

Then I describe my father's incarceration incident. He promised me that he will do everything to release my father, and became very depressed of the issue. After three months of continuous follow- up with great difficulties and much discomfort, finally, he was released on a high bail, and he came home. However, my father was no longer the same man as before. He had lost his health and vitality, and he would often sit deep in thoughts and after four years, he died in Tehran. After that, it took me three and a half years of continuously following up to regain the bail that I had given to the court for the release of my father.

One day, I was invited to repair a large manufacturer of household appliances in Marvdasht near Shiraz. In the section of automatic magnetic airbrush and glazing device they found troubles and it was disabled. I went there and about three or four hours later, I found out what was wrong. Just because I did not have a particular required component, but with a little change in the circuit, I put a similar component and the machine started to work. This factory had been confiscated and the revolutionary guards ran it. When I sent the bill, he was surprised and said, "How much is your price per hour? You have charged us too much for half a day." A day without work at the factory would have cost hundreds of thousands of dollars. I told him, "You do not need to pay me any money at all, this is my gift to the factory." Later, they sent a refrigerator for me as a gift. One of the workers told me that previously when the machine shut down a specialist from Germany came. He worked for at least two or three days, reading instructions and running tests and finally, he did the same work as I have done. His invoice was at least twelve times as mine, also, the cost of the hotel and the trip back to Germany. They paid it with thanks. However, for me as an Iranian expert who repaired their factory fast, my bill was too high. Another time I went with a group in Tehran to the largest copper mine in the headwaters of Kerman during the New Year celebration and we did about sixty-five direct current engines repaired and launched their setup. We repaired and operated the electronic assemblies and we set up nearly sixty- five direct current motors.

One day I was invited to repair in a big plastic factory in Shiraz. They were producing PVC pipes with different diameters. Two parts were damaged and disabled. The first part was related to the machine that produces pipes with the middle diameter, which had the highest sales. They were unable to control the speed of a very strong direct current motor. Luckily, they had completed the control of the technical drawings. The control part, including several electronic control boards, which were all protected with a tough material and sealed were not repairable and embedded inside the engine compartment. Due to the nature of the machine's work and having the electronic drawings, we designed and built another electronic board that was equivalent to the original. In a separate panel which I placed near the engine with a series of cables connecting to the motor, we were able to fully control the operation of this part. When the system began to work all workers sent blessings all the way down to America, they said. What did this have to do with crime of America, I do not know. Next step included several large injection machines with their control panels, which was also very important to the factory, and they had not worked for a long time. I started looking at the electric drawings and tracking the circuits with each of their function. I knew the general information while not all the machines worked because of a malfunction in the main panel. However, in the main panel, a large number of wires that connect different parts were mixed. Finally, after two days, I noticed one wire of some control wires from one section to another section of the electrical panel was connected and with the thin tube protected, one of those wires had been cut consciously and again it was embedded. I had frequently checked there, but I did not have noticed. However, I found it, and I replaced the wire, and the whole system was launched and began working again. It had caused so much trouble because it was sabotaged by a person who entered the device deliberately. The factory expropriated and belonged to the Islamic Revolutions Foundation, and

I had to report to different places the cause of problem. As a result, some of the factory workers were fired. They designated me on the technical advisory board and there were all the companies and industry groups which belongs to foundation, including the Petrochemical and Fars Meat Industries.

Another interesting event, we were invited to the Metal Smelter and Pipe factory in Ahwaz for the installation of the new machine to produce and form iron pipes. Before the revolution this machine was purchased from Germany but not yet installed. According to our visit to the installation place and after seeing the maps of existing devices and their installation information, our offer included a price calculation of all costs to provide them with counseling from professionals and university professors. I also calculated unexpected expenses and emergencies, which doubled the price, and the proposal was sent to them. After a while, a letter came from Ahwaz that said your price is too low, and we prefer to offer the job to a German company, which has more experience. Sure, their cost was ten times the price of our proposal, which they had trusted.

Briefly, in addition to the city of Shiraz, I was invited to other cities in Iran. Sometimes we had to replace a particular piece; we had an electronic board with almost the same specification design and it fitted instead. Much time passed, my company had become well-known, and many Bahá'ís worked for me. The Iranian Revolutionary Guards during the Iran-Iraq war was one of my major clients. I had made a very strong 240-watt amplifier for them that they used for propaganda on the battlefield. Our current location was small and we moved into a basement, it was a large place and had an extra office space.

Over five or six years passed. During this time, my mother got sick and died, and I was deeply saddened. My father then went to my sister's home in Tehran for a short time. Unfortunately, he passes away shortly after that in Tehran, and I was left alone in grief. Parents are the strong pillars, we, children, have relied on them, and our support depends on their existence. Without them, there is no more of this support and you truly feel alone. You do not know what you have until it is gone.

Figure 9—The nineteenth anniversary of our marriage with children Pedram, Pooneh, and Pegah (1989).

Three of my colleagues created an electronic repair company and later when I was informed, I went to visit them with a bouquet of flowers to wish them success in their company. Another of my colleagues established a repair shop. Sometimes he came to see me for advice. He always used to say, "When I worked here, I would soon troubleshoot and simply fix it. Now I have to think a lot, and sometimes I cannot fix it." I always had to help him. I never told him that when you were here, I would advise you what to do and where to look. I was so tired because I trained the people who were establishing their businesses. Of course, this was my first and original purpose and it was a pleasure when they appreciated my help, and if they were proper, they do not promote themselves to bring me down. I had a friend who was a pilot, he had found me an occupation in Dubai. They hired me and they agreed that each month I would work three weeks in Dubai and one week with my choice to live anywhere in the world, with excellent facilities and a good salary. However, I could not accept it because my father was alone in Shiraz and anything I did, I did it for him. He did not agree to come with us to Dubai. Maybe it was an excuse and I really did not want to go.

One of the groups that were members of the Revolutionary Committees were called Guidance Patrols. They worked in groups of four who drove in the busy streets. They were looking for the people in the streets who did not follow the Islamic dress codes or behavior.

Also, those who did not wear Islamic dress and had no Islamic behavior, they caught them and brought them to the Islamic committees. As you know, in the committee, either you are flogged or jailed, or if you could pay enough money, you could go home. Many people were stuck with the persons who had no ethics, were fanatics, and wild. Many people were involved with such people who did not have any human dignity and overzealous. Nobody knows what happened to him or her.

In my company, the women and men worked well together and generally, they did not think about the Islamic restrictions. The guidance group came one day to my office and wanted to visit my workshop. I was sure that if they got into the workshop, some of the staff would be arrested. While I was thinking about this, suddenly two of the Iranian Revolutionary Guards arrived in my office, they were working with us, and I had repaired many types of equipment for them. They told the guidance group "we have been working with this company for years and we trust them. The company is committed to Islamic values and the people who are working here are very nice." The Guidance group said that if this company is trusted by the corps, so we could be trusted too. They filled out a form and wrote that we visited and this company is committed to Islamic values and then they left. Then I took a sigh of relief, relaxed, and thought truly a miracle happened once more, and they never came back.

Figure 10—Obtain a license to use the mark "Good Quality" On all our products from the Ministry of Industry and Standards of Iran

Establishing a Computer Company

Computer science has developed in the world, my brother in Germany sent me a new personal computer with 360 KB memory, 30 megabytes of hard disk, and the Intel 8080 processor. It was one of the newest personal computers available. University and higher education to Bahá'í youths denied their admission, and it was a big problem for Bahá'í families. I held computer classes for the youths in my company. Then I established the first computer company in Shiraz.

In Shiraz, I had a friend who had a master's degree in computer science and at that time, he was a carpenter. I had spoken with him a lot, that he could teach computers, and I wanted him to be a partner in my new computer firm. He made excuses that he does not have enough money to participate. Finally, I bought his carpentry tools so I had to pay his share in the company. Many of Bahá'í's youth used our free computer classes and when they completed the training, some of them became professionals. Most of them were working with us and some of them had their own business. Our work was quite good and we were working for Shiraz University and most colleges and schools. After that, many computer companies established in Shiraz who's our employees among them were also. Of course, it would have been very good if they were true competition but they betrayed me in order to promote themselves. This was very painful. It was said, "Glass is the closest hazardous partner to the stone, so every failure is from the bad companion."

We held the first nongovernmental seminar about Internet and GPS networking at the Shiraz University Library Hall. In this one-day seminar, we took advantage of professors and experts from Tehran. With the implementation of various programs about the basics of computers and their applications in industries, as well its application in medical equipment was an important part of the conference. The use of the Internet to get information on geographical maps that can search all over the world5 9via satellite. Also, a screening of a documentary about how GPS works. In this seminar the electronic mail was presented for the first time in Shiraz, which was highly regarded. After that, a lot of requests were made to repeat this seminar again in Shiraz University with our partnership, and they were very successful seminars.

We also organized the first computer exhibition at the Park Hotel in Shiraz for a week. In this exhibition, I received assistance from the various companies in Tehran. Moreover, we occupied about one hundred and fifty square meters of exhibition hall space. We showed the complete computer facilities and its peripheral, which was unique in its kind in the region at that time, and it was very welcoming to visitors. They came from different levels such as university professors and doctors, bank and government employees, students, and ordinary people that had visited the exhibitions and were delighted.

Figure 11—Apple Exhibition in Tehran Sheraton Hotel.

We had a very successful and well-known computer company and on behalf of the Apple company in Tehran, they suggested that we represent the Apple computers in Fars province, and we welcomed the proposal therefore we finally became Shiraz Apple center. Then we rented an apartment next to our company and showroom where we sold Apple computers. We even wrote several applications including accounting for the Apple computers that Apple was considering and sent several interesting gifts. All of a sudden, unfortunately, after a while, Apple computers in Iran became part of the sanctions by the U.S. government. We were not able to buy directly from Apple company but indirectly from other companies in the Persian Gulf.

After a while, I was sick of too much work and I could not go to the computer company for about a year. My doctor advised me to work only in one company and just in the morning. One day, after about a year in the morning, I went to the computer company and saw that everything had been changed. Then I realized that my copartner (Mr. Carpenter) with our sales manager together had founded a new computer company, and my copartner has had almost all of the company's operations moved. I was so upset that I shut the company down officially and immediately left it. Then they said I was a tyrant and a bad person. That was the results of my serving them for years.

The Biggest Mistake of My Life

God will never put a problem on your way unless he knows you have competence and capacity to cope and the ability to resolve it. If you are capable of doing something well, but you don't do it, it calls a failure. I know that I have made many mistakes in my career but the biggest mistake that I have ever done, I trusted the people who were not deserving because of governmental paperwork, buying the electronic parts, and solving various official problems, that should be conducted in Tehran. Moreover, I could not often travel to resolve those issues in Tehran and particularly because of my faith, so I needed someone who could do this job for me. I had a friend in Tehran who had studied in Germany and previously worked in the Iran electronics industry in Shiraz. I knew him from the past, we also had family relations. He proposed to me to be his partner so that we have some stocks in the company. He could buy the electronic parts and do the official government paperwork very well in Tehran. He could also sell products in Tehran, the products that we made in Shiraz. This was a very good job for him. I thought that he solved my biggest trouble and half of my work. Therefore, I could continue to operate in Shiraz without any stress and the company would be better managed and had more success. Unfortunately, I made the biggest mistake of my life. I agreed with him and he bought some electronic parts with the very limited amount of money as his share, so he was able to become my partner.

I realized that although repairs and factory services was a good job, it was a hard work and had a lot of responsibility for me. I found out that the electric current had fluctuated in Iran and more has been on and off a day. Moreover, electric motors, especially in the refrigerator, would be soon useless. Therefore, I designed and built an electronic device to protect these kinds of motors. When the electric current fluctuated up or down in its marked limitation the power would automatically disconnect from the fridge and take into consideration the time for liquid gas venting, that it was the main cause of stoppage of that type of engine. Then another device to protect of three-phase motors, design and build it. It was a very good job and we became a nationwide manufacturer. We were able to speed up our production and we sold it all over Iran. Although we had fewer commercials we sold our products very well. A lot of people had been copying my design and were refrigerator protection maker. It was interesting that every time I made a change in my design, they would change their design too.

After a while, I managed to buy thirty-five thousand square feet of land in the Ab Barik Industrial Zone with a monthly payment in Shiraz. Factory construction lasted about two years and we moved there little by little.

Figure 12—Eramtronic Manufacturing Company in Ab Barik, Shiraz

Starting over in a new location I began to have many problems. Industrial zone was outside Shiraz and we leased a bus to bring the employees from Shiraz. Then we had to think about their midday meal. The bigger and greater place should have more machinery and features. We had to borrow more money from the banks, so that we could make more profit. We should have produced more products, so we needed to buy more parts. Finally, we had to hire more staff, and we had to organize them quite differently from before. When you hire many people in a short time, you may make mistakes because you do not know them well, and you do not have enough experience either. In particular, people who should have management responsibilities in the organization. Especially in Iran, where most people were obsequious and were unreliable, and at first, they showed themselves well respected and well deserved. Another issue is ethics of Iranian people who always blame others for their mistakes. I am probably guilty of the same practice.

I think that God is always protecting us, even for a short time he gives the people a chance to succeed. It all depends on the person and how he can use this opportunity. I do not know what to say. Being successful requires not only hard work but also a variety of other factors are also involved. Choose your partners wisely, and knowing whom you can trust is another factor. Too much trust and friendship with people who do not deserve it, is the most dangerous factor in failure in business. I think that we should never judge others because we could never be in their position. Maybe we would have done the same thing if we were in their position and place. I am just stating the facts of my comment, finding the cause that's why, and I do not want to be judgmental about the people. Maybe it was all my fault, what had happened to me. However, you know that if an article which was not written, does not have any mistake.

Unfortunately, sometimes a human who does something which can create problems for them in the future and they cannot justify it in the future. Moving the company from Shiraz to the industrial city with this quality and volume, special in the situation ruled in Iran that minorities, particularly the Bahá'ís have no right to live, it was a big mistake. Over a period of ten years after the plant was established with me as the managing director, the company had established an administrative system with the international relations and rules according to the ISO-9001 standards. All of our products were licensed from the Institute of Standards and Industrial Research of Iran. The company's management had covered five sections manager, administration and accounting, sales and purchasing, productions, and also research and development. The research and development section had two patents. The company had sales representatives in the most cities of Iran and neighboring countries as well. Therefore, the company now had a nationwide reputation as well which provoked jealousy of the fanatic people in the state offices and other organizations.

In 1382, Iranian calendar (2003 AD), our company had succeeded as an "Outstanding Industrial Unit" to be introduced in the Fars province. During a ceremony in commemoration of the feast day of Iran's industries, the Fars governor awarded me with the "Token of Appreciation" as managing director of the unit. He also appreciated my efforts and diligence in industries of our country.

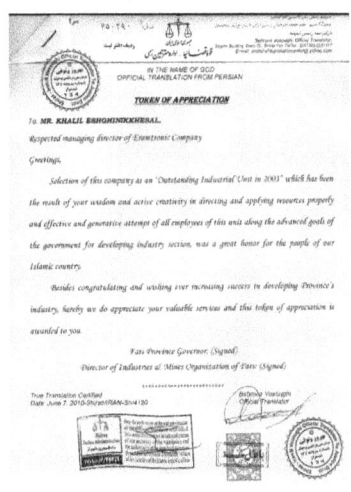

Figure 13—The original of Token of Appreciation Award

Figure 14—The translation of Token of Appreciation Award

This event caused jealousy and stimulation of other companies and religious fanatics in government agencies. They were always trying to undermine and create problems for the company and they hurt me and finally placed a big impact on me. My copartner's abuse and the wallowing of colleagues eventually led to decreasing my level of success in order to bring me down. People began to become negative and tried to criticize me instead of praising me.

Fortunately, I was so busy with different work and solving the problems of the company outside and had trusted the section managers too much, that I had been away from internal problems. My Tehran partner was the manager of the trading section. Also, he was Tehran's sales representative and my production manager was the Shiraz reseller.

These were my biggest mistake that I can never forgive myself. Later I realized that because their profit did not allow to be a reasonable price for company products. My copartner in Tehran that placed the most purchasing for the company should do his duty, he received a commission to buy the goods which were purchased from the sellers. Given that the company's sales were very successful but the company profits were not acceptable. Corporate overhead costs were very high in addition to routine administrative and promotional expenses, the costs to be out of city and employees' transportation expenses, to maintaining a large location and giving many benefits to the employees. Also, large sums for payments to the banks as avail loan which was a large sum, there was no room for the company's profits.

As in an ancient proverb, *the door does not always turn on the same wheel*, it is true and likewise our company did not continue the same as before. I was alone, the others were only thinking of their income and no one was thinking about the company. The company's financial situation had been blocked from several directions. On one hand, the reasons of my copartner and the others the company's numerous obligations to the banks. I was so busy with solving the financial problems and fight against prejudice and evil conspiracies of persons or companies outside of the company, that I was not able to make a correct decision. I had given more authority to my section managers to resolve internal issues.

Fourth Chapter

Factory's Critical Situation

All of a sudden, by order of the government, my business license was canceled due to my religion and I could not export our products, and more importantly, we could not import electronic parts or other raw materials from foreign countries. It was the biggest shock that the government was taking over our company's tired bodies. We had to buy all of our parts and raw materials in Iran at much higher prices. I remember we wanted to open a line of credit to buy the parts from South Korea but because of lack of business license we were not able to import in Iran. Finally, we bought the same parts from an importer company at three times the price. It caused our products to increase its cost. If we added to our sale prices, we could not have competed in the market. It should have sold for a little benefit that it was not useful to our overhead expenses. It means that we were absolutely in disadvantage and we did not know how we survived, and how long we should hope to have profits once more. Our liquidity diminished so we had to fire about fifty employees.

In Iran, employers must compensate fired workers for each year of their service equal to the sum of the last two months of their salary. There were several employees who had worked in our company for twelve or fourteen years. It was a very heavy cost for our company but we had no other choice. With the expulsion of those people, many issues started and also being apparent, and I had realized many issues that I should not have noticed. I was so preoccupied with issues outside of the company and I was unaware of the internal problems.

I found out what happened and understood what was going on but unfortunately, it was too late. A famous proverb says, glass doesn't have any closer friend than stone, so any failure coming from friendship. I seriously felt like I was alone and did not know what to do.

I was surrounded by all kinds of pressure from every direction. I did not know how to start and how to resolve it. On one hand, the company's financial situation did not allow me to fire the persons who had high experience and high salary, on the other hand, I could not ignore their acts. Therefore, I took the responsibility. That was not much, but it would create more problems. Life taught me not to be friends with people who have no values and are unappreciative and never offer them any responsibility and your friendship.

Unfortunately, the person who was responsible for our accounting retired and I hired a person who had a bachelor's degree in accounting and had experience in a large hospital. He was referred to me for this position by the chief administrator of the factory. I found out later that the new accountant previously worked as an accounts assistant and due to misuse of the accounts of the hospital, had been dismissed. After eight months, we received a letter of social insurance based on a failure to pay the insurance of company staff he did not mention in the monthly report to management. Then I realized that he did not pay the monthly employee insurance as well as some sales tax, that it would be three percent of the amount of our monthly sale which was not paid. With the due penalties in eight months is an enormous sum. It was the reason for our decision to dismiss the accountant.

When he was leaving our company, he demanded a large sum of money, which he claimed that had paid for various expenses. Since that time the company was unable to pay in cash, I had given him four checks for four months with very high profits. I remember that some of these funds had been paid with my order. Then I hired a senior accountant with good experience. According to the calculations of the new accountant, he had caused huge sums of financial loss to our company and he ignored and did not consider many of the invoices or other documents. Therefore, the company sued him in court. He had given my checks to the wicked and crime people, and they came to our home address. Two people came to my house at one time who badly behaved and said, "you should give our money tomorrow," and they were threatening me with a big knife. In the following day, we advised them that they come to the factory and take their money (of course the accountant's money).

When my son and my lawyer were informed, they said he did not have any rights to send two thugs to collect money or threaten my family. They advised that next time when they come to get the money, immediately call the police so they can arrest them, and then we will go and file a complaint that they threatened our family with a knife. They will surely go to jail. The next day, the two men came. My secretary called the police, and the police came. I thought that these two men had gone to jail several times, and it is normal for them to go to prison. They had knife scars on their bodies, and they had my home address and they knew my family. I was on the assumption that they will be imprisoned for one year or more often. Then what? Only a few other enemies, they are not even afraid of killing the people. I had enough trouble. Therefore, I told them to give a written declaration in the presence of the police that they would not come to my house anymore, and I got the old checks and gave them new ones. They committed and took the new checks' number and the payment reason stipulated in the undertaking. Police also confirmed it. I said the money is in the account, and they can go to the bank. They went happily from the company, and I did not see them anymore. Maybe it was the best course of action. I do not know. The money of checks would eventually be paid, why bother myself more. When my lawyer heard what I have done, he told me, "why did you do it? They should have been punished." I asked, "At what price should they have been punished? I do not want to increase the risk of being damaged by them more."

Then we got a respond for our complaint from the court regarding our accountant. The court, according to our documents and evidence, gave him the order to pay a large sum as a fine to us. Because he could not pay that amount, the court ordered him to go to jail but I accepted that he only return the owed money that he took from me so that he does not go to jail. My son accompanied my lawyer to the court as my representative. He received a check for the same amount of money that he had owed. The check that he gave to us granted that he must pay by the order of the court. Otherwise, he would go to jail.

Also, we found in court that a few others had complained against him. In one instance, he had taken a loan from the bank with other home ownership document. We found out that he had a history of drug abuse and he was addicted to heroin, and had committed many criminal acts. Maybe I am the only person that he missed, and I have survived. These individuals are like poisonous snakes, affable and hypocritical and with a tidy appearance they attract you and suddenly toxins enter your body, which will destroy your life.

After two days he told my son, "In the account of that check you have, there is no money. Please change these checks to other checks that are fully accredited and in accounts that have enough money and you will be able to get money from the bank today."

My son who was a young and inexperienced person had been deceived, and he changed the checks. It meant that he had paid us all the money. However, about the check that he had given to my son, only the amount of money and date was written on the check and a signature. It was not clear who was the issuer. Whether it was a stolen check or if there was any money in its bank account, this was the question! When I was informed, I did not let my son go to the bank because I was afraid if he took this check to the bank, perhaps this check had been stolen. First, I asked an acquaintance who worked in the bank, who this account number belonged to or if there were any stolen checks reported. It was interesting that there was no such an account number and nobody with this personal profile still had not been born. After a while, I realized that any person in Tehran could buy a check with the fake name and fake account number from any bank you want with any amount of money written on the check, and the check that he had given to my son was one of them.

Later my son sued the accountant because of fraudulent check. He completely denied in court that he has given the check to my son. "This was ridiculous," he said.

However, my lawyer, while he spoke in private with him, recorded his voice. Then he admitted in court that he had given my son the check and he did not know that this was a fake check because he was an anonymous person from the sale of equipment but it was important to us for him to admit that he gave the check to my son. However, after investigating the case and the investigation of banks and other entities, the judge issued a warrant. He had been committed to two crimes; first, he should have given the check amount to my son, and second, checks are securities, the component is public documents, and forgery of public documents is illegal. Shortly after that, my son went to America and gave me the power of attorney to pursue his work. The accountant did not attend the last meeting of the court and the judge issued a warrant in his absence and for his arrest, but the problem was how the sentence was given to him, and how he could be arrested.

This person to be arrested is another exciting adventure that had a separate story. Every time I stopped by his house, either he was not at home or they told me that he is not at home. However, after his repeating arrest warrant three times (because the arrest warrant has specific date). Finally, the judge issued the inspections and entry on his home. I had recruited a person like himself, a so-called gangster, so he could arrest him and handed over to the police station. One afternoon, he, with a police officer, went to the accountant's house by court order and log in, and when he made an attempt to escape to the roof, he was arrested on the stairs and was delivered to the police station. Then I went to the police station. I had taken his first arrest warrant before this act happened. After finding his home address and many times of ineffectively going to his home. Then I went to his sister's home and told her that I'm not going to make any trouble,   I just want to have my money returned, and it is better if he will be done. She said I had to go to see her mother and she could not do anything for me. Then I went to his mother's home, also, she said that she was not able to do anything and for a long time has not any contact with his son. They said that I had to speak with him. It was a lie. I told her I could not find him and I threatened them that I would come with the police officer. Then his mother had spoken to him by telephone and made an appointment to meet me. I went to see him and told him, "You know that you did not treat me well, but I want to give this opportunity to give you. Please, return the money and the additional amount that you took from me, I do not want anything else." He said that he doesn't have any money to give me, besides, he did not owe me. I showed the court order and said, "I can arrest you, but now I give you the opportunity to prepare the money."

He said, "Very well, you give me three days until I prepare the money and I will call you myself."

I told him, "Surely."

He said, "One hundred percent."

His three days took a month and he never contacted me, and I knew from the beginning. I did everything but I could not contact him anymore, so I hired this particular person (gangster) for his arrest.

When I arrived at the police station, his sister with his wife and another man were already there. I knew the man who was there. He was a good man. They asked me to release him, I told them, he should give my money back. Then, I am going to release him, by the way, I do this act because he should understand the result of fraud. Finally, we had argued until eleven o'clock at night, they were talking and talking about, but none of them were satisfied that at least give me a guarantee. If I had left there and had gone, maybe I would get better results, but I could not leave them alone and send him to prison. I was very sad and tired, and I felt sorry for his wife. Finally, his sister told me at eleven o'clock at night, she guarantees that if her brother did not pay me the money, she would pay me the amount. These contracts are written up at the police station and everybody signed it. I knew that she would not keep her promise and I accepted it because his wife was really devastated. I agreed and gave my consent but it was too late. The next day was a weekend and the judge would not come back in the next two days, so he should be in custody at the police station until Saturday. I did not sleep all night and I was worried about him, and the day after, I went to court and again gave my consent. Although his sister did not pay me any money, this event was so hard for me see a person imprisoned although he was guilty and deserved it.

After two years, our new accountant, who was an old man, retired from the company. I learned almost all the accounting methods from him during that time. After our accountant had left, I undertook the accounting responsibilities with the help of a bookkeeper. I was working in the factory from 8:00 a.m. to 11:00 p.m. every day, and my copartner in Tehran was comfortable, and he had a good sales profits, but he had expected that I do not have taken any money from the company. I remember that day in 29th of Esfand (March 20th) which was a holiday, and the next day starts the Iranian New Year and everything was shut down for five days. One of the company's checks was returned from the bank and I should have disbursed it on the same day but I could not, I called my copartner and explained the situation but he said that he is in the northern part of Iran on the Caspian Sea coast, and he cannot do anything and I better find a solution. Yes, I was the person who always thought about everything and had to resolve the problems. So as always, I thought again, and I gave the police station a warranty to pay the amount of check after New Year vacation. I had to leave my home document as a warranty, otherwise I would have been arrested and detained there for six days because the business was shut down. After vacation, my friend in Tehran did not even ask me anything about this incident. It was my life at the time. Sometimes people have pretty thick skin that they endure all the hardships.

The financial situation deteriorated day by day, and we had all kinds of debts, a large amount of money was paying only the interest each month. It was a long time that the installments of bank were overdue. The point was that the bank, according to their rules, warned us, we have three months' time to pay our debts with their interests, and they sent two auditors at the cost of our company. The situation was very critical and my copartner in Tehran in the time of eight months did not come to Shiraz. He did not even call me once.

When I asked him a question, he would answer me that he cannot tolerate the discomfort and in the meantime, he cannot do anything. I was lonely with huge troubles and nobody wanted to help me. The situation was unbearable for me and I did not know what to do. Finally, with the mortgage of my personal home documents, I guaranteed to pay the other bank and pay the part of the company's debts to save the company. This ended the bad disposition and additional fees. However, I must say the most of the time my home title document was used as tool to guarantee the money for the company's debts which was in the mortgage of banks. We needed to think of a solution. When the situation was quiet and temporary issues had been resolved, my copartner came with many suggestions from Tehran to Shiraz. A man accompanied him who had a shop on Lalezar Street in Tehran. Lalezar Street was an emporium for electrical appliances. I have had no more information about him. They offered me if the company would elect this man as a representative of our products for all of Iran, he would pay the monthly bank debt payments and the employees' payroll. I had no choice but to accept their offer. After long negotiations, the entire agreement with him had been closed, and I introduced him as our representative in Iran.

However, I have to say, later I realized that this man was a friend of my copartner and together they had arranged that they were going to share all income from sales. Fortunately, I had added a clause in the contract that in the first six months, each of the parties could stop the contract with a notice. This was the only usable paragraph and a good suggestion that I had taken at that time. Over the first three months, everything passed well and from the fourth month, Shiraz's expenditure not provided completely with various excuses. I found out that all income derived from the sale of the company belonged to Tehran, and now the company, due to miscellaneous expenses, only losses. According to my calculations, they had a huge revenue in the first six months and the company had a lot of losses after. Then due to our agreement, I find a way to cancel the contract. As I said, they had already thought about it, and they also had a solution. They knew how to push me to continue the contract.

Maybe you think why I always realized too late, and why I did not check it out before it happened. First, let them do it and then think about alternatives. A director at this level did not permit to make this type of decision. These are just the ineptitude that was completely my fault, and I totally agree if the situation was normal. I was lonely and very tired, as well as having many problems that surrounded me. All around me were a bunch of friends and colleagues who were only thinking of their benefits, and even consulting with them was harmful. I worked at the factory fifteen hours a day, so I did not have more energy to think accurately and timely. Unilaterally, cancellation of the contract brought many problems for the company and me. It was really unbearable and unexpected. We bought many raw materials, especially after canceling my business license bought completely from Tehran, and my copartner had done this task in Tehran. In order that my copartner would be able to purchase them, we opened a bank account in Tehran while alone, my copartner or me, could sign the checks, but the pledge was with both of us.

One day, suddenly I received a letter from Mr. Representative that caused many problems and even changed the future of our company. The letter contained many interesting issues with the new offers, also enclosed the photocopies of six checks with the huge amounts of money, which were signed by my copartner from our account (my copartner and me) in Tehran. The amount of money was about the total value of our factory. In the letter it was mentioned that the money was the amount that my partner spent for the purchase of goods and raw materials for the company were borrowed from him, and my copartner has given these checks as a guarantee of payment. If I do continue to cancel the contract, he would force to take his quest to take checks from the bank. He has also a brother who is a mullah and very influential. It is much better to continue the contract, and he will adhere to all his promises.

I was in a very bad and sad situation, I wanted to scream loud, but the sound did not come out of my throat. I wanted to say, how could it be possible that my copartner whom I've worked together about thirty years, and we were friends, our families were close together, why did he so greatly betrayed me. I thought about it a lot, and I had consulted with everybody and got intellectual assistance from them. I did not know really what was right and what I had to do. If I wanted to continue the agreement, surely the company will be disturbed, and if I wouldn't continue it, how would I pay such a large amount of money and why should I pay? Finally, my lawyer offered a way out. He wrote an agreement letter and said, "If your copartner sign this agreement, you will no longer have responsibility for the payment of these checks." But I was sure he would not sign it. So we thought about a solution— how we could ask or force my copartner to sign it.

Decided to Sell the Factory

Before I got the letter enclosed with my copartner's checks, nobody could even talk about the selling a part of the company shares with me. I had liked it as a child because I had grown it with a lot of work and efforts in thirty years of my life. However, from the receiving date of that eventful letter, regretfully, I understood that I could not keep the company in this condition. I was starting to talk and consult about how to sell the entire company or a portion of its stock. I wrote a letter to this content to my copartner. "Dear friend and copartner, after thirty years of friendship and partnership with you, I realized that we can no longer continue our partnership together and the company's financial situation is very bad too. The experts should evaluate the factory, either you buy it or I have to. Another way, we should find a third person who will buy the factory with the evaluated price. Then we do not have any more debts from the banks and other debt issues and we are free to do anything we like." However, he did not even answer me. When he was in Shiraz, I had followed this issue, and finally after much talk, we wrote a written agreement. I would start by factory expertise and I should check out how the total value of shares to transfer and find someone who would buy the factory. He told me he did not take my letter seriously because he knew that I loved the factory and he was in thought that I was never satisfied to the selling of thirty years of my efforts.

The manager of the quality control of our company was a young engineer from a prominent family of Shiraz. His family was Muslim and wealthy, and he was an intelligent and polite young man. I often asked for advice about the company's issues with him, I consulted with him this time too, and asked his opinion, and I offered him to buy some company shares. After a while he said he is ready to buy the shares of my copartner, if he does go out of the company. However, I knew that my copartner would never accept it. So we should not tell my copartner who wants to buy the factory.

First, we should think about the checks and then we talk about the sale. For this reason, my son-in-law suggested to me that it seemed logical. He told me, first of all, that I should give him a complete power of attorney. Then we all, with the young engineer, went to my son-in-law's home in Tehran, and my copartner and his son also came. I should point out that my son-in-law's family had an apartment in a nice neighborhood of Tehran. If one of the family members required staying in Tehran for a few days, they could stay there. On the appointed day, we all went to Tehran and my copartner and his son also came, and we began to discuss the company's future. By the way, I had brought along two copies of the agreement that my lawyer had written.

We all came together in that place, and discussion about the company and its problems started, which was very exciting. Many proposals were given and also offers were provided with many solutions, but none of them could solve the company's problems. Then I told them that I could not have more responsibility of the managing director of the company. You can choose another person as well and specify his legal salary. The salary that I had received was not enough, and my salary for this responsibility to someone else is too low. Suddenly, my copartner said that I did not have any expenditure in Shiraz and did not pay rent, I am in Tehran and have a lot of expenses, and also I have to pay such a huge rent. I should point out, that his rented apartment was in the most expensive place near to king's palace in Tehran. He said that I should not have earned any salary because you do not have any expenses in Shiraz. My son-in-law could not bear it anymore and said, "You spend too much money and have an expensive apartment or Khalil has no expenses in Shiraz, what is the relationship in between? Tell me first, what does the issue mean that you, in favor of your friend, has given these checks?" He showed the photocopy of the checks.

He was surprised and said, "I do need to have money, and he had given it to me, and these checks are for his money back guarantee."

My son-in-law said, "You did need to have money, why didn't you give your personal checks to him?"

My copartner surprisingly said, "I did need the money to buy raw material and equipment for the company."

My son-in-law angrily said, "Why didn't you mention it in your report to the management, why was it not entered into the company's accounts, and why such a huge amount of money? Why? Why? So these checks are illegal and you should afford to pay them yourself. My father-in-law does not have any obligation to pay them." Then he showed the power of attorney and said, "Look at me, Khalil has given me full authorization and I will sue you. If I should sell this apartment and spend its money on the court for sending you to the jail, I will do it. Therefore, you would understand that is not easy to fraud." And he went to the main door of his apartment and opened the door and said, "Get out of my home and see you on the court."

My copartner was so surprised because so far we have never had such an encounter, he had always treated him with respect. Besides, he knew well that if something goes to my son-in-law, he runs it will, he was shaken and scared. Since he was from the neighboring city of Isfahan, I mean Najafabad. Najafabad is a village near Isfahan. The people of Isfahan are known to have a bluffing character that at first, they will be very hard and bring pressure, if you retreat and accepted, you lose. However, if you showed a more severe reaction and refused them, then they would retreat with your acceptance, you win. My copartner did the same and said, "Tell me what I have to do to make you happy."

Immediately, my son-in-law said, "Nothing, you just have to sign this agreement." And he put the agreement in front of him and my copartner signed the agreement without reading it. Then my son-in-law told him, "Please put your fingerprint." Then he put the ink pad forward, and he had his finger inky and fingerprinted on the agreement, I also signed and did the fingerprint, after that all attendees at the meeting signed and fingerprinted the agreement. Then we all went out and went home. On that day a miracle happened. Later my copartner found out what a mistake he made but it was too late. He was always thinking about it, how he can find a way to compensate that event. I have been saved against checks, and it was a matter of principle.

Auditing for Transfer of the Company

After the checks problem was solved nobody talked about it. But I have heard that my copartner's wife said that she did not expect the bad behavior we did to her husband. She claimed that my son-in-law and my son were so rude to her husband, and my copartner was very upset because he was like their father, and they should treat him with respect. They are in a lower class family and they are not raised to be polite, they also don't know the meaning of respecting someone who is an elder. Of course, they already apologized.

As I noted earlier, they are following the frequent commutes between Shiraz and Tehran. I finally got an agreement as special bailiff. First, the factory should be fully evaluated by various experts. Either my copartner or I would purchase the other party's shares, or find a third party to purchase the whole or a part of the shares of the company. The company was evaluated by four different experts and its price had been identified, but in the worsening economic situation in Iran at the time, who wanted to buy a fragile and broken company and would be willing to pay this amount of money? The issue was that the company owed a large loan to the banks and this could be useful when the buyer does not need to pay a total amount and could pay with the long-term installments of the bank. The main problem was that the people did not want any partnership with my copartner. They were saying that he lives in Tehran and he cannot be positive in Shiraz. Furthermore, my copartner did not want to sell all his stocks. However, I was ready to sell, but there wasn't anyone who wants to buy my stock. I had talked many times with the young engineer but he was saying he was willing to buy if his mother and he could buy sixty per cent of the company's share. They wanted to have the complete control of the company. Then I had to promise him that for a whole year I will manage the company and he will always be by my side until he has been fully trained. He will determine the factory's price by himself and the value of the plastic molds that my copartner in Tehran had purchased was too high, he only calculated half of the purchase price, some equipment were old, he could not accept them. Briefly, the price that he was willing to buy was very low, it was approximately the same as our debts to the banks and determined by his lawyers. I had no other choice but to accept his price because the Persian New Year was close. I had to pay the amount of two month's salary as the year-end bonus and New Year's festal gift to the employees. I still owed them two months of salary and the bank payments were due, so we need to decide quickly. I could not speak with my copartner because he would never talk to me about the bad situations and specially this event. Indeed, I had to make a decision alone, and I did it.

I remember, it was two or three days before our New Year, the young engineer provided a statement that we would sign. Then he could give us money that I could pay to the employees as well as the bank payments. It was nearly noon that the young engineer with my son and I went to Tehran by car. Shiraz is about a thousand kilometers far from Tehran. We arrived in Tehran at about one o' clock in the morning and went straight to my copartner's home and they were waiting for us. His son-in-law was also there and after many negotiations finally he signed the statement, according to the contract the buyer should give to me the amount of the calculated money as a director of the company. Then we drove to Shiraz at about 3:30 a.m. We stopped in the city of Isfahan (between Shiraz and Tehran) and we rested there for a few hours, we arrived in Shiraz the next morning. Then I went directly to the bank and got the money, with the hand full of money went to the factory and paid the employees their wages for four months, they were very happy, and they went home to celebrate the New Year.

I went home very tired after about thirty-six hours of discomfort, stress, and insomnia. That time, no one asked me if I still have any money with which I can buy a New Year gift for my children. The point was that the company employees' children were happy and had a great New Year celebration. I could not express my feelings and now that I am writing these lines, I feel sadness and in a strange situation that I cannot describe it. It reminded me again after several years, and it is really painful. It was very difficult that after thirty years of hard work and effort, it was easy to lose it all and could not even buy a New Year gift for my wife. I had always been saving to develop the company and I did not even go for a fun trip over the period of thirty years. New Year's holiday was over, how could I go somewhere that I had established and I had grown it with hard work and much effort. Yes, what a great dream I had for it. My heart was really in pain and I wanted to scream but I knew that no one would understand my feelings and would not see my tears at that time. I was laughing and pretending to the employees to be happy. I explained to them that the company's situation had changed now. The young engineer has bought more shares of the company but I am still the director of the company and there is no threat to fire the employees. I changed my office and moved to another room. My ex-office was repainted and had new decorations and was prepared for the young engineer. I brought my office equipment to one of the other rooms next to my ex- office where I had stationed. This time was one of the hardest and most painful periods of my life.

An agreement between my copartner and I was to clarify the financial position account based on a written treaty. Each person was responsible for his personal debt and also all expenses, the income will be determined by each individual and the difference between the total revenue and the costs per person that determined the amount of the debtor or creditor of the person should be paid accordingly. Therefore, we created two accounts. The first was Tehran who related to my copartner with all his expenses and revenues. The second was Shiraz that related to me with all my income and expenses. I had identified the total accounts and were calculated by an accountant. The calculation show the difference between the debtor or creditor of the total amount of incomes and costs of each partner was determined. One of the partners had to pay the other who has spent more costs or has less income compared to his.

Then my copartner with his son-in-law who knows accounting's law came to Shiraz, and they did a full audit of the entire accounts, and they took the copy of all the calculations with themselves to Tehran. After a week they came back to Shiraz and again the accounts were reviewed, almost all of the accounts were accepted and some of them rejected. This issue happened three times. Finally, after several months and after three times of full review with all the company accounts, they had not accepted some of the Shiraz costs and I accepted their proposal because I wanted to end this situation. Then we closed all the accounts. Therefore, the amount of the debtor or creditor of each partner were identified and according to our agreement, I should pay a sum equal to (for example X RLS) my copartner so the accounts will be perfectly completed and cleared. Then I gave to my copartner a check for the same amount that we had agreed and all the accounts had been completely closed. Unfortunately, I had forgotten to get a receipt from my copartner, also, there was no debit or credit between me and him. My copartner agreed that the accounts be closed and completely pony at the last step. Then he took one CD with all the company final account details for the third time, and he brought it with him to Tehran. It should note that all the funds for the purchase of shares that the young engineer had given to me, I had brought them as Shiraz income. I thought that all my problems had been solved and there were no more excuses for my copartner. I had written in the check "this amount of money is the ending of all accounts and the company's pony" which I gave to my copartner. Unfortunately, I had forgotten to take any receipt from him to the settlement of all accounts between ourselves. Usually, when we write a check with the name and subject as the same, it, in itself is a receipt, also the company auditor for his report to the board had recorded all things. However, when someone wants to make an inconvenience, he will find a way. If I have written a personal note from my copartner, who has agreed that all accounts had ended and there is no longer any personal account between us, there were no more any excuses that it will be placed. I am extremely sorry that I didn't write any, indeed, I hadn't even thought once my copartner will abuse it in the future.

My copartner, for the first time after the transfer of our company, had come to Shiraz. The next night, when the factory was closed, he entered the factory and made a key and entered my office. Why did he do it? Maybe he knew better. This issue caused many problems for the company and especially for me. Also, the company's new management had to change all the factory locks and it was an intense distrust for all. The incident brought more problems including the replacement of factory guards and a few other things like the installation of CCTV cameras that for the employees were unexpected. However, my copartner was proud of his behavior, as a result, he could not go to all sections of the factory, he only had permission to go to the limited parts of the accounting section and later this issue caused many problems.

We chose the weekend holiday to install CCTV cameras and the other devices. The next day, before the factory begins to work, the staff commotion began, they questioned why we have CCTV installed unless we do not trust them and we want to control them. A few staffs resigned, including the company product manager, and some of them were with me from the start of the company. At first, I did not understand this kind of behavior. Then I realized that all the issues had been stimulated by the product manager but a few hours later they withdrew their resignation. I had spoken with the product manager, that's why and I asked him to be deterred from doing so and he did it for me. Now I wish that I did not have this action because the young engineer was upset and said that this was a good opportunity for the product manager's dismissal. He had been working with the product manager for years at the same level of management and he knew all his behavior and actions that I did not know about. I am sorry that I believed him to be so simple and honest. I still could not understand when you do trust somebody why would he want to betray you and take advantage of your trust. When someone fails, the others without any regards to events, conditions, and outcomes calls him a loser. It is true that he is a loser. However, if you want to judge someone, first, put yourself in his place, live with his sorrow, his doubts, his fears, his pains, and his laughter. Remember, everyone has a destiny. Then you can judge him.

I grew up in a family where lying was very bad as well as deception, duplicity, and wickedness were unforgivable sins, and we did not really know what was their meaning. We have heard nothing but love and kindness from others. We had learned in the ethics classroom that we should be friendly and helpful to others as well as helping others is a part of worship. We also studied that truth is the principal source of a human being's life and that kindness is a glory of light. In the world outside of the home or ethics classroom, these have no meaning. At least where I had lived, there was a different concept of human virtues that prevailed.

My wife and my return to Iran was a wrong decision. Perhaps, I had no other choice. My residence permit in Germany was expired and I had to renew it, also a very good job at Iran Electronics Industries had been offered to me in Shiraz. More importantly, my father insisted that I go to Shiraz because they were lonely and my mother was sick. I did not know that when I go to Iran the Islamic Revolution will happen. After the Iranian Revolution, I found many good jobs out of Iran, for example, in Australia they even send for me a plane ticket but because my mother was badly sick and my father was lonely, I was not able to go there. After my mother passed away, I found a very good job in Dubai, which I could go for a week every month anywhere in the world to live with the good salary and excellent facilities. Again, I was not able to go because my father would not come with us to Dubai. He said, "Your mother is buried here, I will be buried here too." He was depressed and sad, and it had intensified my father's imprisoned issues because of his faith. I could not leave him alone with those issues. So I stayed there. Maybe this was my destiny, I don't know.

I was well known and at that time because I had developed my business. I had what I needed, but I was very simple- hearted and trusted everyone. I had been thinking that if you help somebody, eventually someday he would compensate your kindness. I didn't know the people who did not know the meaning of kindness and friendship. You should not give them your affection and trust or even help them. Maybe it was a big mistake, but I did what I had been trained and it was my nature and character. I had trusted those who betrayed me and I had given my friendship and love to those who were wicked to me and most of all, the conditions and my surrounding as a Bahá'í in Iran led me down and eventually lost all the fight. Although I should have known the present situation in the Islamic Republic of Iran that a religious minority could not have a factory with a lot of worker and facilities and Iran was not in a normal situation. Cancellation of my business license means cutting the lifeline of the factory. You could not purchase the raw materials from abroad and also cannot export your products. However, if my friends didn't betray me, I would have never been so badly broken down. Sorry to say, I have learned that much friendship and love are very destructive and brings many expectations. Unfortunately, I have realized this issue too late. It is okay, I did my mission as a human being at that time. Although I had been much hurt, I have polite and successful children, which are the most valuable fruits of my life. They were not hurt too much but my wife who has always accompanied me in the happiness and sadness was hurt, because of this issue I will never forgive myself.

Fifth Chapter
Events After Company Transfer

After a while, the first new board was formed with the participation of all stakeholders. Then the company auditors gave a full report that was based on how the company has been transferred and its problems. He has also described that he has closed all the old accounts and opened a new account from the beginning of the year to all of the partners, and he did also add a summary of all information related to the company. Then he resigned from his position as an auditor, and he left the meeting. The chairman and managing director were selected and a new auditor. The young engineer had been selected as a formal managing director. The board also approved that I should manage with full authority the company unofficially, and he will work with me as a trainee for a year. We were working with the new company management without any debts and with the convenience went forward with the correct programs.

My son with my son-in-law, together they established a computer networking company. At that time, in the Islamic Republic of Iran, the only way to get a higher education for the Baháʼí youth was in online education from the universities or institutes abroad and it was limited, the computer sciences were one of them. Since the start of the Islamic Republic of Iran, all Baháʼí students had been expelled from all institutions of higher education and universities. The Baháʼí youths were no longer allowed to enrol in any tertiary institution or teaching in any way and all the Baháʼí professors had been dismissed from their job. Therefore, my son and my son-in- law learned computer science in major networking online and they received an online training courses in Cisco networking and Microsoft. They always went to Dubai to take exams and to register, they gave my sister's address in Germany because the Iranians have been sanctioned to take these exams. My son did more than three years of continuous study and much effort and received many books from Germany through my sister and finally, he graduated and achieved success. Then he, with my son-in-law, established a computer networking engineering company. They offered networking classes and had a sales department. They had some well-known equipment sales representative from abroad. Their business had been running very good and more institutions and people who were working with the networking issues had been working with them. They had an office in the best part of Shiraz, this place was also the center of computer and Internet companies, and many people were working there.

Soon after my children had established their company, the office of the Friday prayer leader[17] of Shiraz has prepared a list of the names of all Bahá'ís who were working in the Fars province. On the list were the names of my son, my son-in-law, and mine. They sent this list confidentially to all the places and said that people should not have any dealing with us and working with us is unlawful. This list was very bad for the people or shopkeeper who was working on their own name. We all worked through the name of the companies. Although it had created many problems, it was not too serious. I think two or three years later, they collected a list again which included the name of all Bahá'í companies. The list had been sent to all government departments and agencies, banks, and also notified to private companies and factories in the Fars province that to deal with those people and their companies were unlawful and illegal. It was the reason that my son and my son-in-law had decided to leave Iran and came to the United States of America. I think less than a year after they handed their company and through Austria moved on to America.

Later, I think four to six months after we had checked the audit and pony between us (my copartner and me), the Department of Finance and Economics sent us a letter asking why we did not pay

---

17   Friday prayer leaders in each province have the power higher than the governor of that province.

our three percent sales tax completely for a few months. In Iran, the manufacturing companies must pay three percent of total monthly sales to the Department of Finance and Economics in addition to paying their income tax each year. We should pay this amount of money which is deposited into a special account monthly and we already calculated and paid. After searching and investigating, we found out that my copartner who had previously presented the company in Tehran produced a device similar to ours with the same name and he sold it with the company's invoice. It created a big headache for the company and myself.

I have to say, after the young engineer obtained company management, we had been traveling to many cities in Iran such as Tehran to meet the vendors and buyers. When we talked with the raw material suppliers and our sales representative in Tehran, I realized that my copartner was getting a percentage of purchasing from the vendors, he also gained a ten percent profit from the sales of the company products. I really didn't know, yet I understand what a huge income my copartner had and this was an enormous sum of money. At that time, I realized the motivation of his insistence to hold down our sales prices and why were our products cost were too high, I also understood why it didn't matter to him to harm the company. These issues had caused much discussion for the board and they made the decision that first, the company should be purchasing the raw materials directly with their vendors. Second, the Tehran representative must be a company or a person who has an electrical shop in Lalehzar. So, in general, all of my copartner incomes had been blocked. He thought that I am the cause of all these issues. This issue was an addition to his previous hatred, which he had toward me, and these issues have multiplied, and he was trying anyway to harm and hurt me.

Thus, my copartner begun to search to teasing me. Later, about two years had passed, I heard from the Tehran representative that my copartner had been complaining about me to the Zarghan court because of the fraud. This issue was heard by our Tehran representative from my copartner's son who was working for him, that I would be in jail in the next few days. Because I had been called up to the court twice, but I did not go there, and the third time I should instantly go to prison. He immediately reported by phone the matter to us. My lawyer and I went to the Zarghan court near the plant site on the same day. My lawyer introduced me to the judge and said that we had not received any summons and we are here to make an appointment. The judge that was a good man said that if I did not introduce myself for two more days, he was obliged to issue the warrant because this was a criminal complaint. However, I was released with the guaranteed placement and then we made an appointment until I, with my lawyer, came to court and defended my case.

I was lucky enough that I found out this issue on time. I have to say that in Iran such a bad event happened which caused many problems. A person who was not even guilty until he could prove that he is innocent will be imprisoned for maybe a year. In Iran, you could pay some money to the communication officer and he could rip the summons and tell the court that this person was not at this address, and he has stuck the summons on the door, or the wrong address will be provided to the court. We had several trial meetings with my copartner with the presence of our lawyers. At the first trial that we were all present, my lawyer told the judge that my copartner's claims against me could not be true and Mr. X cannot verify because the last check that he has received from me, he confirmed that his account is refined, also between his and my accounts had been completely refined. He told the judge that the check had been for company accounts, adjusted and refined, but I never signed any paper or said our personal accounts were refined. He indebted me personally and he should pay me (my copartner) such a sum of my share from the factory's selling price. The judge appointed an expert and the work offered to the experts to an investigation. I gave to the expert all bills of the factory's sale and all relevant documents as well as the expenses. The experts confirmed that my copartner didn't have any proof that I owed him. However, later my copartner claimed again against me on legal court in Shiraz. He claimed to the Shiraz court unlike his words in Zarghan, he told in the trial that I did not give him the company shares and I also manipulated the firm's account and took money illegally from those accounts.

A few months passed, in the last trial session, the judge's ruling was that this is not a criminal issue since no fraud occurred. If my copartner still has any objections, he could bring his complaint to the public court and the trial has declared the end of file in Shiraz. Then the court released my guarantee. Of course, it was not what my copartner wanted. A few months later he complained to the public court in Shiraz and Zarghan again. He was saying that I, as settlement administrator, did not pay him all his company shares sold to the young engineer and his mother. It is a long story while it happened I will explain later in the following sections.

Perhaps more than eight months passed from the ownership changing in the company, I was continuing my work and was a little bit relaxed, and the only thing that bothered me was I was far away from my children. Really, if they could be next to me, they would calm the pains that my copartner had caused so I would not feel lonely. Although there were people who were very kind to me, I, at that time, could not trust anyone. The company was going forward and the young engineer attempted to grab a business license. He was a Shiite Muslim and seemed to not have any problems. The business license was necessary for the company and we could buy some cheap raw materials from other countries, we could also export our products again and could have a great benefit for the company. The business license was issued by the Department of Commerce and they told him that he should have fired all Bahá'í employees. Again, other problems and much headaches begun. Many Muslim employees had already been working in the company. The accounting section were all Muslims they were also in other sections but there were still many Bahá'í employees working there.

Most of the Bahá'í staffs thought that was my fault and they blamed me that I had promised them that they should not be dismissed. Iranians say, "Again all bowls and jars were breaking over my head." In other words, I was being blamed for everything and it was totally my fault, I created all of these problems. The issue of expulsion and the business license, I had to keep it, so long that my promise to one-year managing the company was completed, and I did it. Of course, the young engineer collaborated and waited. Unfortunately, I could not tell them the deportation subject because of being Bahá'í but they did understand it, why?

Finally, I found a way, and I told them that everyone would be redeemed. The company would pay them two months of the last salary for each formal working years. Also, depending on the amount of years that they have been working, they would be getting the unemployment insurance for a three-year period. Also, those who want to stay with the agreement, they could, but they should be waged as daily worker and no insurance. However, how much they had worked, it will be rewarded, but they could not go to the court and sue the company. Surely, it will get worse for them because they could not get the unemployment insurance. However, some of them went and complained to the court, and as I told them, they were not entitled to unemployment insurance because they were Bahá'ís. Some of them were happy because they had a good amount of money accrued and they could establish a small personal business, or buy a car and work as taxi drivers. Some of them remained there and started working happily as pay-per-day worker. Some others were also stimulated by my copartner and they began to hurt me, which I will explain later. One of the employees who lost his home in the Iran and Iraq war moved to Shiraz. I hired him, helped him, and trusted him. He had a special character and I had a particular interest in him and send him to work in the warehouse. He was responsible for outgoing all the products from the warehouse and he would have to confirm them. I often helped him as a good worker because I knew that he has children who were going to school. He was going to retire from the company. In Iranian law, when an employee is about to retire, the company pays him at least one month of his last salary for each year of working. I calculated the number of years that he had worked in the company and paid him but he complained to the court that the company should pay him a reward for working hard. I was the company representative in court and after much discussion, I accepted. We paid him a sum of money as a reward. Suddenly, he said it was much better if he was in Evin Prison since he had worked hard for this company and this company owed him a lot of money, and it is his right because he did work well for years. Evin Prison is one of the most dreadful regime prison. Due to this thread, I said that I am sorry but I cannot accept that our company pays him any reward and the judge accepted my decision, we did not owe him any additional fees. He only got the amount of his pension. I didn't tell anything about

Evin Prison to the young engineer and what he said in the court. I just told him that we do not need to pay an extra money to this employee because he knew that I always had extra attention to this person, and he would be always flattering me.

When this person came to the company, he pleaded that he lost his job and his employer did not pay him any money accordingly. He came from a city where the war has destroyed. He had a wife and children who needed to go to school and he needed to support them. I hired him and he was very thankful and told me that he always prayed for me, which I had made a place for helpless people. However, now he has such as strange behavior and speech in a formal trial. I didn't know and could not believe that the previous remarks were all only a game and flattery. Well, now he is my enemy and everywhere vilifying about me, this is really painful. Sometimes a man asks himself, how is it possible that a person who had loved you for several years, now that you could no longer do anything to him, became your enemy, and he did vilify you. *Maybe it is a little example of how the Islamic Revolution of Iran was created.*

Unfortunate Event

There were two sisters in the company who were in the war- torn village KhonJ between the Abadan and Bushehr. At the time of the Iran-Iraq war the Iraqi soldiers surrounded the city of Abadan. Their families had taken refuge in Shiraz. They were in a very bad financial situation and one of my friends introduced them to me. I hired them. At the time of hiring, I told them, "This is the law of our firm, the first six months to a year you are a trainee and when I see that you are doing well, I will hire you officially. They happily agreed and started to work.

After eight or nine months, I officially hired them, and they worked as an electronic montage worker in the manufacturing section, and they worked fine. A few years later, their financial situation had been good and one of them got married. They were completely satisfied until the issue of selling the plant and laying off of employees happened. They were like the rest were redeemed as well as the three years of monthly unemployment insurance and they were day laborers who worked in the factory. A few months later, I had no more formal job in the company and only went there to visit sometimes, I was trying to accomplish and solve the problems for my pension insurance since I had not been insured myself in the years when I started my job. I needed to have a few years to complete my retirement. Finally, I could bring the time when I had worked in Iran Electronics Industries, of course I spent a lot of time and much more troubles, so I could complete my pension requirement and retire.

One day, when I was in the company, these two sisters came to me and told me, "When we started to work, and that is about seventeen years ago, we started to work when you didn't officially hire us and according to this we have lost money, you should pay us this amount of money."

I answered, "You agreed and were very happy at that time and if you did not agree to work why did you accept it? Only you did not have medical insurance but with the other issues, you were just like everyone else. Tell me, what have you lost, and what is your problem?

She said, "We want our money and we will sue you."

I said, "Do whatever you want to do." She knew that complain about the subject happened seventeen years ago that is not useful but it can be very harmful. Afterward, I realized that this issue related to my copartner been revived.

A few days passed and I have forgotten that case. I was at home one afternoon, the house alarm went off and I opened the door. Suddenly I saw them, two sisters, with a robust bearded man who was wearing a black dress. He said, "We came here to get their money from you."

I told him, "They could go and complain to the court."

The man said, "I don't need to complain and I earn my money on my way." He wanted to enter into my home. I didn't let him in and almost closed the door but he became involved with me and my shirt was torn. My wife, Farahnaz, came forward and asked what is going on, suddenly the man's tight fist that wanted to hit me, hit my wife's face. With the help of my wife we were able to close the door and I immediately called the emergency police and asked for help. Then I called a few other friends and our son-in-law's family who immediately came to our home and the police came too, we all went together to the police station.

We filed a police complaint form for trespassing and assault especially since my wife complained about what happened to her face. The police officer arrested them. The company production manager went to the police station but I did not tell him to come. He begged me to not complain and said, "They made a mistake and they will apologize and regret. You are a Bahá'í and maybe they take advantage of this opportunity, it is much better to resolve the matter between ourselves, and it is better to give your satisfaction. I promise you, I will pursue this case, and they will be punished in another way." Unfortunately, I accepted his words and gave my consent and they were released. At the time we were going out from the police station, the man dressed in black said, "We will finally take the money from this person." I didn't hear his words but my companions did. We all went to my son-in-law's mother's home. My wife was feeling extremely bad and constantly crying, her face little by little turned black from the bruises.

That night, when my son-in-law's sister's husband came home and heard about the case and saw my wife's face, which was swollen and blackened, he was extremely upset. He said, "Why did you give him the satisfaction? This person should be in jail." Then he, my wife, and I, immediately went to the police station to have our assailant arrested again. If we did not consent the first time, the police would arrest him, everything was much simpler, but now the issue is different, he was no longer at the police station. For arresting him, we need the court's order, and we should follow the law. So the police station at first sent us to the coroner's office to prepare a report of how much my wife and I were damaged. It took four days and cost us a lot of money to determine the injuries and medical report along with pictures of my wife and I. Then the police officer sent along with us the coroner reports and the report of police history about how it happened to the court. We had an appointment at the trial court and we explained all the facts, the judge was extremely upset that this man put his fist to my wife's face, he made an appointment for the following week. He said that this man would be punished hard and a week after that we should go to court with this person, he issued an arrest warrant for him.

When the girl and her brother (the man in a black dress) have been informed of our complaint, they tried to talk to all of my friends and family, they asked for help and said that they were provoked and they did not know. This was madness and the were hoping to get forgiveness and sent flower bouquets and pastry to my wife as an apology. Even a person who I had respect for came to me and told me that they understood how bad was this kind of behavior and also it was a great mistake. This person never wanted to hurt me and especially my wife.

Also, what is to gain with imprisoning them and maybe it will just harm our society. It is better to forgive them.

I told him that they should attend a meeting with a few friends and several of their colleagues. They officially apologized to my wife. Also, they would bring the amount, which I have given to the coroner and court fees, this was about the same amount of money that they wanted for me to pay them. They came one day before the court trial and they had done what I asked for. The session was held in my home a day before trial in the morning. In addition to one official workers' representative and two of the factory staff, many of their relatives and friends and several of our friends participated—a total of twelve people. The official workers' representative said in his speech, "When we had any problems or someone needs to have a job, he has been assisting us and I have not seen anything else more than the good name and human being from him. We are extremely grateful for the many years of good cooperation." Then the man further said, "We are ashamed of our behavior and we're hoping for forgiveness." He gave my wife a bouquet of flowers and to me the amount of money that I had set and apologized. I got the money and offered it as a gift to the Orphan Children Organization. The session ended with tea and cookies and prayers for my wife.

The next day we went to court, the person also came, and my wife gave him consent. The judge was surprised and to the man said, "You are very lucky that these individuals are very good human beings. If they do not consent, I will send you to prison for at least three years. Also, if it happens one more time even, they give you the satisfaction the court will imprison you." He solemnly promised and in court wrote and signed that he would no longer create such problems and the case was closed.

After that we found that longer living in Iran was useless and even, I might go toil anytime. My children who were living in America were very insistent that we also go to the United States. They have sent an affidavit of support letter to us. All our friends would recommend to even acquaintances and us that we should go there and we should leave Iran. Therefore, we thought about coming to America and live here.

"Finally, the young, pious, and kind engineer confiscated the rest of my share. With this excuse, I have to pay my share of the costs of the dismissal of employees and previous company insurance, as well as the percentage of the share required to increase the company's capital. He knew that I could not and would not be able to pay such sums, so he owned all my shares.

Saying: A bird goes after a cow to find food and suddenly gets stuck in the dung that threw at him. The fox sees and saves the bird, then eats the survivor and happy bird as a delicious morsel."

Sixth Chapter

Prepare to Get Out of Iran

Figure 15—The last photo we took with our children in Shiraz, Iran. First row from left: Pegah, me, Farahnaz, Borna (my grandson)
The second row left: Pooneh - Pedram - Parisa (daughter-in-law) - Parham (son-in-law)

As I said earlier, my staying in Iran was very dangerous and I needed to go abroad. I had enemies, like my copartner who was going to destroy me with a full force. There were also many people who were very opportunistic and waiting to be able to take advantage to use this situation. My children, by the help of a company that has headquartered in America and Austria, sent us an affidavit of support letter to get an American visa from the U.S. Embassy in Vienna. They also opened a case for us in that company. First, we had to fly to Vienna in Austria and from there to get the visas to America. Then from Austria we flew to Los Angeles and from there to San Francisco where my daughter was waiting for us. This took about a year and a half that we were able to fly to America. While my house in Iran was still on a bank mortgage and I was also indebted to the bank. I needed to pay the money that I owed the bank for them to release it, I asked my brother in Austria for a financial help. My brother helped and sent me the required amount. We also had to pay the foreign company the sum of eight thousand five hundred dollars for the expenses of transferring our cases, so we could fly to America. I borrowed the money from my sister in Los Angeles and my brother. Everything was then ready for us to move to the United States. At first, I had to think about my house, if I don't sell it, surely it would be confiscated after I get out of Iran. The sale of the property at that time had a very bad condition and I could not sell it, hence, in the first phase, I did transfer my house to my wife's sister. However, it was possible that she would be going overseas. Then I sold my house to my daughter-in-law's mother, and I started to sell my home furniture and items.

My copartner was somehow informed that I was going overseas. He began to investigate how he could stop me from going to America so that he again could sue me. Again, he had chosen a proficient lawyer and sued me in the court of Shiraz. He told the court that I am running away to America and the trial court should start as soon as possible to prevent me from escaping the country. I remember that day was the birthday of the Bab, the court had made an appointment for us that I had to be in court on that day. That day was supposed to be a very great day for me. The Bahá'ís celebrate this day and are on holiday that I was present at court. I was very sad, upset, and disappointed, that I wanted to scream. I asked my lawyer, "What did I do wrong to him that he wants to bother me in such a way?"

My lawyer told me, "What did you say? What had you done to him? You did the biggest blow to him. You had stopped him from stealing and blocked his good income, which in his opinion is a great sin. Again, you say, what did you do to him?"

In court, the trial judge read the text of my copartner's complaint and told us, "What are you going to say?"

My lawyer started to talk and reiterated what he had said in Zarghan court, he repeated it. He continued and said, "According to the documentation and official expert reports my client is innocent and has not committed any crime."

Then the judge turned to me and asked, "Do you want to go to America?"

I told him, "Given that my kids are there, I want to take a trip to visit them."

My lawyer said, "It is a short trip. If it will be necessary, during his absence I would like to present in court as his lawyer."

The judge, after investigating the case and listening to my lawyer's speech, said that according to the documentation and in a short time he could not order a banning exclusion for me. However, I had to guarantee the court that at the end, if the court found me guilty, I would report to the court. Then the judge ruled to determine an official expert to examine this topic. After the trial, I talked to my son's mother-in-law by phone so that she would bring my house documents and title as a guarantee to the court, this lasted until two o'clock in the afternoon. My copartner was very happy that he now could seize my house but he did not know this document was not in my name anymore and he could not seize it. However, he could and also was able to bring me in a great destructive psychological situation. My lawyer promised me that my copartner could not win in this process. I should be completely comfortable and the judge had to make such decision. He assured me that my house documents would be released soon. Then I went home very tired and weak. The court introduced two official experts who work with my lawyer and his lawyer together to provide any documentation.

I was thinking how could a human be so selfish, who wants the other humans for nothing be destroyed. I do not know when, but was not too long time ago, I saw a movie about a person who was very rich and selfish that if someone did the slightest movement unlike his desire, he was ready to set a farm with all its inhabitants on fire and destroyed them until a sense of his self-seeking would be removed. I thought at that time that it was just a movie scene and those only happens on films. In addition to that, in all the stories we heard or read, the good guys always succeeded. I said to myself that finally the story should be written otherwise there was no story. Of course, here I do not want to talk about the good person or a bad person and I never said that I am a good person or my copartner is not. The only issue was, why such a behavior, which is far from human dignity. On the assumption that I am a sinner, so what? You, as a good person, why would you do those inhumane actions. Especially him when he showed himself as a follower of the ideas of friendship and affection and he grew up in a family with good customs and secular. Would it have been better if at first, we would speak together without any inconveniences and solve over issues ourselves. Maybe that was much better and the issues had been resolved between us a long time ago. In the past we both, fortunately, agreed and closed our accounts. Why does so much insistence and pressure? What do all these excuses mean? Why have we placed our distress on others? Why have we ignored the thirty years of friendship and cooperation? I am so sorry, I don't understand this hostility.

As I said before, the Shiraz trial judge had introduced us to two experts, and we could contact them to hand them out all our documentation. One day my lawyer and I went to their office, we're to give them our reasons and documents. They said they are still waiting for my copartner's documents. He did speak with them by phone but they did not yet have any evidence of his problems. It is better that they again call him to ask when he could bring his documents. So the experts spoke by telephone with my copartner and he said that he has given all the documents to his lawyer so they should call his lawyer. When the experts contacted his lawyer, he said my copartner has been talking a lot, but he has not still given me any documents. Then the experts told us until my copartner does not provide his documents, they cannot set their report. When I asked how long it would take, they said it could even take more than six to seven months to stretch the time out, until they prepare the reports. They continued and said, "If he gives us his evidence this week, we will be able to provide our reports to a maximum of three weeks."

Furthermore, my copartner wanted to gain a time as long as I was out of Iran. Maybe he could take advantage of my absence in the court trial, and he did it.

I do not know how much time passed, I didn't have any more power and no feelings, and did not know what would happen. My father-in-law fell and broke his hip and was taken to the hospital, and there he had a surgery. Unfortunately, after a while he fell once more and broke his pelvis again but this time, he was very weak and he could not move his foot again. Later he was also diagnosed with Alzheimer's disease and was refused admittance by any private hospitals. The public hospitals were too indifferent and had the large rooms with a minimum of ten to twelve beds but only one chair for the accompanying person. Most days I had to go there and nurse him. I was having problems with my work and myself because I was the only man in the family. They needed me to resolve their issues and take care of my wife's father at the same time. Although at that time I could not concentrate well, I had a lot of tolerance and could handle the difficulties as well. My wife's father died at the age of eighty-six after nine months of suffering.

I talked about the accountant who gave my son, Pedram, a fake check and what happened after that, the subject of his court's sentence and his arrest warrant, I had completely described. Well, I do not know how long it was but after a few years in this strange situation and extremely busy—I was surrounded by many problems—I had completely forgotten about this issue. Suddenly one day, a letter came from the court to answer some of the questions and I must go to court No. 47 in Shiraz. The subject of the complaint was my previous accountant for slander who was filed by my son Pedram, which was not in Iran then, I was representing him so I had to go to the court instead. If I had really, at that time, didn't have mercy on this dishonest person and did not give him my satisfaction, he would have been in jail now. A poet says, "If you see a blind next to the pit, it is a sin if you don't help him." Now I say, if you help him who does not fall into the pit, it is a sin. These are all my fault, trusting him and my generosity toward him, thirty years of my life wasted. I went to court on the appointed day but my accountant did not show up but his lawyer came, he was not a good lawyer but he was close to the regime. The judge read the lawsuit and asked me what do I think. In the request they said that my son is a fugitive. He has made many accusations against Mr. Accountant who has brought him a lot of notoriety defamation of character. My son should be paying compensation for his actions, as well as many other claims. I told them that first of all, my son is not a fugitive, he traveled with a formal passport and permission for schooling and all the travel documents indicating that his travel is legitimate. Second, I am not a lawyer who knows all legal issues but I know that all of these claims are unrealistic and did he have any evidence to prove his statements? Then I told the court about the checks issued and all the things that happened. I also said that because of my consent, he is not in prison now. His lawyer said that was one of the reasons why I slandered him. If I was right, why was I instantly satisfied and why did I not get the court decision on the validity of my right.

I realized it is better if a person who knows the legal issues would speak and defend me. So I said, "I request of the honorable court, let me join next meeting with my lawyer to court, so that he will, according to rules and documentation, defend me. The judge accepted my suggestion and made an appointment for the next two weeks. Then I, with my lawyer, went to court to defend me.

However, two weeks later, my lawyer went to court with all documentation including previous court orders according to his tricks and checks and its issues have presented. The court order on his complaint was unacceptable and the story ended but this time my lawyer got an obligation that he would not, in the future, make any complain about my family. Therefore, he could do both material losses and too much wasted my time and above all the other trauma and mental distress to me. I am flabbergasted and could not understand it, what was the issue, what have I done, again they want to find a way to hurt me. This increased my motivation to decide to leave Iran. Indeed, I was afraid of everything including my own shadow.

I had no extra time, I was very busy selling all our home appliances. Fortunately, I could sell my car for a good price because it was an old Chevrolet and did not have a lot of clients, only certain people wanted it. The buyer determines the price of my car himself and I accepted, I was really happy if I sold half of this price. Another interesting story was to sell our home appliances. Many different people who came to buy some things to our house were familiar to us. They thought that I should give them these things free of charge or paid very little money. They thought that they were doing an extraordinary act and they were very merciful to me. For example, a person who was very kind to me and was always appreciative, we also have a family traveling together with us. If it was necessary, we always helped each other. He had a photography shop in a very good neighborhood in Shiraz and also has a lot of homes and property. He did lend money to people with a high profit. I often borrowed money from him and he gained a good profit from me. I liked him because he was affable and very hilarious, most of the time we confabulate together. One day, he came to our home and chose some of the crystal glassware, which I had a very cheap price calculated for him. He told my wife that he picked them because he once guided me an advice, otherwise, he does not need them. My wife was very upset and told him, "If you were saying that you should give all these things as a gift because of our friendship, maybe I would do it, but for what you told me, I am so sorry, I cannot give them to you." He left our home with discomfort and never returned.

We sold our appliances slowly. I had more than eight hundred books, which include reference books, dictionaries, historical and religious significance as well as economic and technical issues, and even interesting novels. I gave most of them to my friends as a gift. I think only the reference books and exquisite books of famous poets and some of the historical books with the minor prices were sold to my acquaintances at the beginning when we were selling our home appliance and facilities. I do not know, maybe everyone thought that we had not paid any money for their purchase. Until the last day, on our flight date, we were still selling the items. I gave what was left of the things to the person who has a shop selling second- hand equipment. I told him, "God bless you if you want any money for these items and you donate to the charity fund."

And we moved toward our destiny.

We were scheduled to fly from Shiraz to Tehran and after two days we were going to fly with an Austrian Airlines to Vienna. Previously, when I went to Tehran for work, I did not call anybody in my family because I was worried that they would get upset that I did not visit them. Also, my two sisters, my uncles, aunt, cousins, as well as other friends, were all living in Tehran. I remember my wedding celebration was attended by about four hundred people in Tehran, which most of them were my close relatives or dependent to them. Now when I go to Tehran no one is there to invite me to their home because of fear of the regime. In all five continents of the world I have family and relatives but I have nobody in Iran. Indeed, most of my close relatives are living in Los Angeles. First, I didn't know where to go in Tehran then I remember that I had a friend in Tehran who was a good friend during my studying in Germany and we met each other and were together most of the time. His family was very prominent and the old aristocracy in Tehran. I talked to him by telephone, told him that I don't have a place to stay in Tehran. He told me that we should go to his house. When we got to Tehran, we went to his home and his family was very nice to us. After two days, we went from there to Tehran International Airport until we flew to new our destinations.

As we went up the stairs of the plane, I thought about what had happened. Why are we going to leave our native country forever? Many thoughts surrounded me and I was confused. It was not our first trip but this trip had no return and we were leaving our homeland forever. From a lifetime of worldly possessions, we were carrying only two suitcases each. We sat down and the plane took off. I was still lost in thought when my wife told me that we passed Iran's border. I felt as if I had been deported from my own country. My heart ached. I was depressed and sad and disappointed with much of life. We had to build a new life in a new country with a different culture and language. We were no longer young and we did not have the youth's ability for careless or even calculated risk. However, we also had no choice. If my brother had not helped us, we would never have been able to make the trip.

My wife and I had to stay in Vienna for a while. It took time for Austria to prepare a visa that would allow us to travel to the United States of America. I was severely fatigued from the stress of leaving Iran and it was a good opportunity to rest and relax. My brother and his wife had lived in Salzburg for a long time. They were waiting for us when we arrived at the airport in Vienna. I was very happy to see them. We all went to my brother's house in Salzburg.

Figure 16—Vienna's airport arrival, my brother is on the right.

Salzburg is an old town with gorgeous green plains that are peppered with small lakes. It is the birthplace of Mozart. My brother's house sat atop a hill with a magnificent view of a green plain dotted with sycamore trees and a distant lake.

We stayed with my brother for about a week and then went on to Vienna where the U.S. embassy was located. We had to stay there while we waited for our visas.

We lived very comfortably and effortlessly in Vienna because we were temporarily staying and nobody did anything to us. We were informed that my wife's brother who lived at the beginning of the Iranian revolution in Berlin, Germany, was diagnosed with the advanced bone cancer. This issue had him very concerned. So, we decided to have a trip to Berlin because we had a Schengen visa so we could make a trip to Germany too. We traveled by train from Vienna to Berlin and for two weeks we were in Germany with him. My wife's brother's situation was very bad, the cancer from his lung has spread to his leg bone and the doctors could not do anything for him. My wife was very upset that no one could do anything positive. My sister and her husband lives in

Berlin, we also visited them and at that time we were together most of days. However, we could not have stayed in Berlin for more than two weeks. We returned by train to Vienna. Of course, my wife's mother and sister came to Berlin from Iran. Unfortunately, after six months, when we were in America, he passed away at the age of fifty- two.

We flew to the United States in June 2011. We flew from Vienna to Zurich (Switzerland) about six hours, and after about twelve hours' flight from Switzerland to America, we arrived at Los Angeles Airport. It took us eight hours to go through immigration and customs at the Los Angeles Airport before we finished all the work for our asylum.

Then we met my son and his wife at the LA Airport. We then flew to San Francisco and arrived at eleven o'clock at night and after almost thirty hours of traveling we arrived at the San Francisco Airport where my daughter, her husband, and my little grandson were waiting for us. We all went together to my daughter's house is Walnut Creek near San Francisco. The next day we moved to an apartment that my daughter rented on our behalf. We began a new life in this city, which so far continued.

Figure 17—Visited my son and his wife; at the Los Angeles Airport.

Figure 18—Arrived in San Francisco Airport (6/7/2011)

It is now about six years since we have emigrated to the United States. Here we have relatively a quiet life. After our arrival in America, my copartner again abused my absence in Iran and complained to the Zarghan court. He accused me of stealing his money and the company's money and escaped to America the Great Satan. Although I had a lawyer, he failed defend me. My copartner could obtain the verdict in his favor. Afterward, I could not even claim that the litigation was not fair. He wanted to seize my house, fortunately, the documents were on another person's name, and he failed. He realized that I would receive a pension and he could block it at court. My lawyer tried hard so that my copartner could only withdraw a quarter of my monthly pension from my account. Now I do not know how long will we survive. Maybe God knows. In addition, my copartner had requested the amount of eight hundred fifty million riyals from the court and the court approved it. I think in the world in which we are living, sovereignty is only in the hand of the idiographic world. This is the world of evil and the human virtues in this world do not have any meaning and concept.

Epilogue

Of course, life does not consist only of disturbing memories. There are so many occasions in our life that are very good and the people are happy. There were also many moments in my lifetime when I was full of success and happiness. Memories of our mistakes and problems which make up stories. While the problems often remain in the memories, the good memories always pass by so fast. For this purpose, in most stories, happy memories always ended too soon. I had learned, from the stones that were thrown to me, to build the firm steps to success and climbed from them and I also did it. I was successful in my career even when I was as a religious minority in Iran, where I did not even have the right to live. From zero financial support and a room in my parent's home, I did build a three thousand square meters plant with hundreds of employees. However, the last stone was a power of the mountain and has thrown from a few directions to me, which has thrown me from the top to down. Ok, it is life, and I can only say who I am thirty years older. I am glad that had my mission is done and happy and that my health is maintained. What was amazing, if I might leave alone for a few minutes, was the ability to be a true dream when I could enter into a state of real survival, into a state of blankness, into a quiet place, painless and peaceful, where I could hold all the times of the world.

By the way, have you ever asked yourself, what is destiny? In the dictionary it is defined as "the things that will happen to someone in the future or the power that controls this." On the other hand, in Wikipedia encyclopedia, we read, "destiny or fate is a predetermined course of events. It may be conceived as a predetermined future, whether in general or of an individual. It is a concept based on the belief that there is a fixed natural order to the cosmos." It is out of our discussion. If we denied overall the fate and say that we should build the future by ourselves and we have complete authority. Alternatively, we do not have full authority on things such as birth and death, the fate is out of our control. On the other hand, I think to be more reasonable, we can, according to the physical and the locative conditions, be in partnership with our destiny and build our future toward them.

I think this is not fair to say, this is my destiny and doing nothing positive for our future. We must be accompanied with the existing conditions to find a way of life and make it purposeful until we build our future and do not ever stop trying and persevering. If you don't reach your goals because of some situation, don't worry and don't be frustrated. However, you should try to share your destiny with the existing conditions, and as much as possible use this situation to your advantage. For example, a person who was born in a country that is under the pressure of superstition, war, terror, and bombing you cannot compare it with a person who was born in Sweden and has all the facilities, and says that his destiny had been made, that is not fair. We should change the circumstances—all human beings were born equal. Superstition and ignorance are all the human miseries. Otherwise, if the people have been taken advantage of their wisdom and consciousness, destiny itself is never been bad. We must change the situation and build our future with better conditions in our favor. If we can.

In retrospect, I think how lucky I was that my life should have converged on history and with the revolution. The revolution which was for Iran and the Iranian people have paid all so heavy a price, and they are still paying. However, it was necessary to bring the people a growing of thought and as a result, the society will progress. The adventure of being able to use my life to help my community, to educate youth for acceptance of responsibility, as well as to improve the financial strength of the community by creating jobs for people who need them, these issues are beyond the measure of joy. That was impossible if the Islamic revolution didn't have happened. Until that time in my life, only I had an experience in the design of electronic circuits, means a soulless work, hardware and logical. I was dealing with the logic and arithmetic and nothing to do with the emotions, love, or kindness to others or fighting with them. I had never thought that I would get involved in such real adventures. Obviously, now I know that in such a condition, I will the same thing but with more experiences and precautions. I am glad, however, that the experience was very painful yet informative, and I am so happy now that my family, all of whom, are successful. I think the most happiness is that we are the witness to the success of the fruits of our lives, meaning the success of our children. Life is a business, until you don't give, you will not gain anything. I have given thirty years of my life to be a witness of the happiness of those whom I love.

When you carried your memories, you would bend your back under them. However, if you put them under your foot, your height will be taller. I, at this moment, bring it out of my heart one after another and put it under my foot to forget them all.

I am a bird of Heaven Garden, none of the terrestrial world. From my body a cage was made for a few days.

~Rumi

Acknowledgement

I thank my wife of almost forty-five years, Farahnaz, for her support and understanding of the issues that I have worked on this book. Her quiet and steadfast encouragement made all the difference as I labored away in my home fondly known as the bunker. I could not have done it without her, or without the love and needing of our children, Pedram, Pooneh, and Pegah.

My parents trained me and taught me when it was necessary, that I could be able to heal the pain caused by unemployment and financial income of those who needed to be helped.

My brother, Djalil, who was my hero, and fugleman in my life. He had always guided and helped me at all the stages of my life and was also a good advisor.

Special thanks to Mr. Frank Mofidi, professor and instructor of English language at the Adult Schools in Walnut Creek, California, for editing my writing.

www.ingramcontent.com/pod-product-compliance
Lightning Source LLC
Chambersburg PA
CBHW051220120626
46547CB00013B/1435